EMBRACING
reMARKable

A FAMILY'S STORY OF COURAGE, LOVE, AND HOPE

EMBRACING
reMARKable

MARKUS BACHMAN
AND
DEB BACHMAN

Printed in the United States of America

ISBN: 978-1-946195-65-4
Library of Congress Control Number: 2020912197

Cover Design & Interior Book Design: Ann Aubitz

Published by FuzionPress
1250 E 115th Street, Burnsville, MN 55337

DEDICATION

We dedicate this story to God and the amazing village
He has given us.

A special shout out to all the employees and volunteers at
Children's Minnesota and Texas Children's Hospital. Thank you
for all you do.

To our family and friends who supported us during our
darkest and brightest hours, a thousand thanks.

To other families on the path of caring for and raising a
child with major health issues. We know, we understand, and we
send you our love.

FOREWORD

We are all familiar with the expression, "one in a million." It refers to someone or something quite special. It is a phrase that we don't use too casually. I met a one-in-a-million young man over twenty years ago in the Neonatal Intensive Care Unit (NICU) at Minneapolis Children's Hospital. His name is Markus Bachman. Markus was born with a grade IV laryngotracheoesophageal cleft. It was discovered shortly after birth when he was noted to be in respiratory distress and required intubation prior to being placed on a ventilator for respiratory support. One of my partners, Dr. Maynard, tried to place a breathing tube through Markus's vocal cords and down into his airway. The breathing tube wanted to move posteriorly, not advancing normally down the airway. Dr. Maynard suspected that Markus had an airway abnormality, likely a cleft or a fistula. He was able to selectively intubate Markus's left mainstem bronchus, effectively providing ventilation to only the left lung. This intervention was critical because, in the hours that followed, Markus was discovered to have a grave airway lesion, a cleft from his upper airway (the larynx or voice box) running the length of his trachea (his windpipe) to his carina (a division of the lower airway to the right and left lungs).

The incidence of laryngotracheoesophageal cleft is estimated to be one in 10,000 to one in 20,000 per live births with type IV clefts comprising less than 3 percent of that total. This type of cleft is the rarest and the most severe. There are case reports from the last thirty years of patients surviving with a type IV cleft, but the literature available at the time of Markus's birth showed a fatality rate of greater than 95 percent. Markus required immediate surgery to repair his cleft. Think of his airway (larynx and trachea) and his esophagus (the muscular connection between the throat and stomach) as two separate tubes that lie on top of each other through the upper portion of your chest. These tubes are separated from each other by millimeters. They have distinct functions that we typically never consider during the course of a normal day as we breathe, eat and drink, or talk. Markus had those two structures essentially filleted open with no ability to maintain the integrity of either structure. Any formula he would drink would go to his lungs, and the air that he would breathe would distend his stomach.

He was taken to the operating room in a matter of hours, where Drs. Anderson, Sidman, and Soumekh were able to close the cleft, creating two separate channels that did not interfere with each other. Markus remained on ventilator support and was fed intravenously. He had several other problems associated with his type IV cleft. He had microgastria, a very small stomach that would not accommodate normal volumes of food. He required a feeding tube to be placed through his stomach wall and down into his small intestine to permit formula feedings. He also had a poorly formed takeoff to his right lung and compromised development of lung tissue downstream from that takeoff. He was essentially surviving with the use of just one lung.

Markus had multiple surgeries during his first few months of life. He was discharged home at five months of age on vent support and tube feedings. He has had over sixty surgical procedures and multiple hospital stays for issues pertaining to his cleft in the years that followed.

It has been my privilege to be his pulmonologist (lung doctor) since his discharge home from the hospital as an infant. I have lost count of how many other healthcare professionals have expressed their astonishment that Markus has survived and thrived with a type IV cleft. He was able to wean off the ventilator and eventually had his trach tube removed at age 8.

Despite his numerous surgeries and hospital stays, he has not let his medical condition interfere with his life. Markus is a young man who enjoys hunting, fishing, bowling, cars, friends and family, etc. I have watched him handle his hospital admissions, surgical procedures, and clinical visits with an extraordinary amount of patience and grace that young men his age do not typically possess. He is mature beyond his years.

Over the past twenty years I have gotten to know his family quite well. His parents, Mike and Deb, are uniquely dedicated to his health and well-being. They have been with Markus every step of the way. As Markus has gotten older, they have appropriately placed more responsibility on his shoulders, empowering him to make decisions for himself. They are models for parents everywhere. His older sister, Heather, and younger brother, Noah, are always supportive of Markus when he has an extended stay in the hospital. The Bachmans are a special family.

Markus graduated from high school and is currently a college sophomore pursuing a business major. He has a part-time job on his college campus. I enjoy seeing Markus in the pulmonary clinic for routine follow-up. As a pediatric pulmonologist, I typically do not have the opportunity to follow a patient for twenty-plus years of his/her life.

I always enjoy my conversations with Markus, although, as a college student, the subject matter can get quite heady at times. He is a humble, focused, hard-working young man. He is the living embodiment of *carpe diem*—seize the day. Markus lives every day to the fullest. He is the one in a million.

~Michael Pryor, MD
Children's Respiratory and Critical Care Specialists

TABLE OF CONTENTS

CHAPTER 1
Markus: Email Revelations

When life hands me a day that my lungs draw breath without great effort or both legs move without weakness, well, it's pretty dang amazing! Yeah, I have health issues. Who doesn't? I am 17 after all, and well, stuff just happens. I did not think my life was such a big deal until one day when my grandma randomly handed me a big blue binder filled with old emails. It should have had some kind of yellow warning tape with a giant bright red "Proceed with Caution" sign on the cover. The plain blue binder contained letters written during the first year-and-a-half of my own life. Things that I had never heard about came to life in front of my eyes. Reading them sort of made my mind explode. Like literally, my eyelids opened up three times larger than ever, and inside my head something detonated, leaving my brain scattered in lots of tiny unconnected pieces inside my skull. Kaboom! Uh, what just happened?

That was my reaction after reading only the first two pages. Yes, two terrifying pages. How many times can one person almost die and yet survive? I knew so little about myself—what life was truly like both before and after I was born. All the uncertainty, the fears, and yet, the joys, I had brought for those who knew me. I have never acknowledged the entire story. I most certainly will never fully comprehend every component, and I'm okay with that. Certainly, at least now I am aware of sufficient details. Even though my focus is on the wide-open road ahead, it's helpful to know what's in my rearview mirror.

Many people have mentioned that I have every reason to question: "Why me?" Truly, it is not something I have dwelled on often because it is not a good way to go about living. Every single breath is a gift, and I am determined to maximize and enjoy each one I am given.

Prior to my entry into this world, Mom had spent an entire month on a high-risk pregnancy floor at Abbott Northwestern Hospital. Full-on contractions had begun by thirty-two weeks. Labor had to be stopped because my underdeveloped lungs were not yet ready for this world.

"Lung numbers are not even in the ballpark," the NICU doctor informed my parents. The thing is, my folks knew something was off with me before I was even born. I couldn't swallow the amniotic fluid, and this made Mom's belly swell beyond huge, like she was carrying at least triplets. But, nope, it was one baby floating in a large private pool of amniotic fluid. A belly can only get so big, somewhat similar to filling a water balloon. Due to the excessive volume Mom was carrying, labor pains came too soon. Amniotic fluid drained from Mom's uterus and IV medications postponed my birth, allowing precious time for my body to continue developing. For a month, she was kept on hospital bedrest, which included constantly receiving intravenous magnesium sulfate and shots to delay labor.

Mom and Dad both knew something was different about their son, me, but they didn't know exactly what, and neither did the doctors. The specialists had talked about the most common cause of this happening, but no one could know for sure. "Very fixable," were the words spoken multiple times before my arrival into this world. We think with ultrasounds and all our fancy medical tests that we can know everything for certain. Nope, some things have to wait to be seen, and many always remain a mystery.

Born: 7:45 a.m., May 26, 1999

After a long month had gone by, the number protocols determined my lungs were developed just enough for me to be delivered, and the anti-labor meds were stopped the evening of May 25, 1999. The next morning at 7:45 a.m., May 26, I was born. You know how when your child is born, you have a smile and are brimming with joy at the fact you have another family member? That was my parents—but only for a few moments. Then fear, sadness, and reality set in. I looked normal, beautiful my mom says, and then the brown fluid bubbled out my mouth while I cried an extremely hoarse, weak sound. Soon I was working extremely hard to breathe, and my cry continued to be raspy. Dad followed the medical professionals as they steered my isolette through the half-mile underground tunnel to Children's Hospital. After running a few tests, the answer to my problems was clear: a laryngo-tracheoesophageal cleft type IV. This was the most severe form, the gravest form, my parents were told that day, of the "very fixable" possibilities my parents had heard during the month before I was born. My stomach was small, roughly the size of an almond and my trachea and esophagus were fused together as one common tube down through my right lung. People need two separate tubes—one required for breathing and the other for eating. I was given quite a slim chance of survival, *in fact, almost none.*

Yes, any parent would be devastated by this type of news. How were my folks going to tell Heather, their four-year-old daughter, that her brother would probably die? Or that he may never make it home? No parent wants to face this potential reality with any of their children, ever. Yet, mine did.

When the doctor gave the grim diagnosis to Mom and Dad, two options were placed before them. Whichever they chose, they were assured, no one would judge them. The first was to do nothing, and I would certainly die. The second was they could send me into surgery to try to somewhat correct what was wrong. The surgery had never been performed at Minneapolis Children's Hospital. I was flat out not expected to make it out of surgery alive. Dad was the one who spoke up, and through his tears, he said, "Please give him a chance." *It is gut wrenching for me to imagine the parents I know and love so much experience such anguish because of me.* I am immensely grateful for the absolutely life-changing choice they made that morning.

Pediatric surgeons at Minneapolis Children's Hospital cleared their schedules and strategized a game plan to save my life. The first procedure began at 3:00 p.m. I was all of seven hours old. Alive 420 minutes, how do I even start to wrap my head around all that occurred in less than a typical workday? It does not even sound possible, and yet I know the intensity of it all only increased as my next twelve hours consisted of four separate operations. This surgical marathon lasted until 3:00 a.m. the following morning. Twelve hours of high-risk surgery performed on a brand-new infant, me.

May 1999 (Dad's email)
We knew that his chances of simply surviving the surgery were not very good, and watching them take our baby completely broke us. . . .

My stomach churns, and the three-ring binder starts to feel so, so heavy. Should I have read this stuff? Babies born with the severe type of cleft that I had usually do not make it out of the delivery room. That should have been me, but yet, here I am. Somehow, I made it from the delivery room to Children's Hospital, to the operating room and back to the NICU alive, all within my first twenty hours. Before going to surgery, my parents chose to name me Markus, which means "mighty warrior." They believed I would have to be a fighter to even survive my first day. Scientifically unexplainable, I did survive. However, my battles had only begun.

CHAPTER 2
Mom: My Second Child

The skin stretched so taut over my heavy abdomen carried a sense that it truly was close to tearing. The telltale "this is getting really uncomfortable" waddle seemed to start much earlier than with my first pregnancy. "I must be farther along or have more than one in there," I calmly thought to myself. And yet, when I turned onto my side, this baby floated down, stopping only when contact was made against my strained flesh that rested on the mattress.

At a thirty-two-week checkup, the doctor's eyes bulged as she caught sight of my belly. Concern and shock evident in both her face and tone, she asked, "Why *didn't* you call me?" I had called. I was told it is quite normal to have back pain and think you are huge during pregnancy. Yes, but this time the symptoms did not equate to typical. As it turned out, neither would his birth.

Two days after that appointment, I was in labor. Nurses scrambled around me, reminding me of childhood cartoon characters, their feet scurrying, with a singular intense focus in their eyes. Maybe it was the drugs flowing into my veins, maybe not. This was happening to me, to us. Twenty-four hours later I was transferred to the high-risk pregnancy floor at Abbott Northwestern Hospital. Then for one month, I alternated between lying on my left and right side in a hospital bed, my extremely large belly resting against the mattress. Listening to Twin Cities Christian radio, 98.5 KTIS, filled the time between strenuous rolling-over episodes.

High doses of magnesium slowed everything. My hands shook, my eyes struggled to focus, and my speech tended to slur. Occasional needles inserted into my uterus to drain amniotic fluid allowed me to breathe deeper and lessened the intensity of the contractions. The interventions allowed our baby to grow and develop inside me for four additional weeks.

Within hours of turning off the month-long anti-contraction intravenous medication, my water broke. Not a trickle as with my first baby, this time there was an audible pop as fluid rushed to fill and then overrun the sides of the hospital bed, creating a waterfall that pooled on the floor. I was soaked from shoulder to heels, lying in puddles wherever my hips rested on the bed. Looking down, my midsection was just a soaked mess, and did not even look pregnant anymore.

Seven hours and forty-five minutes later, we briefly celebrated our second child, a son. His hair would be soft and curly, I could tell. The shape of his small face was so similar to his sister's, exactly as it had appeared on the ultrasound. Now I witnessed the evidence up close, the dimpled chin, cute little nose. He was beautiful. "Is that a cry?" It was so soft and hoarse I had to strain to hear his almost-silent wails. Brown saliva bubbles covered his lips, popping and appearing with each cry. I had no idea what this meant, but in my gut I knew. . . *it was not normal.*

Spoken words became impossible for me to decipher, as if cotton filled my ears, muffling everything. I could see mouths moving, but nothing made sense. Weeks earlier, the physician, a newborn specialist, had assured us that the most common cause of unborn babies not swallowing amniotic fluid was "very fixable." I held on to my belief that doctors at a children's hospital must have seen every kind of situation possible. From what I did understand, the doctor was able to pass a tube from our little boy's mouth to his stomach. I thought that meant my baby was okay.

Mike hesitated by my side as nurses started to wheel our son through the tunnel to the NICU at Children's Hospital across the street. "Stay with him," I told Mike. He kissed me and followed our son out of the delivery room. The rest of the birthing process was completed with my sister, Denise, by my side.

The delivery room nurse pushed my wheelchair to neighboring Children's Minnesota Hospital via an underground tunnel. The gray walls held rows of large pipes. My eyes struggled, attempting to adjust to non-fluorescent lighting. My head, heavy from exhaustion, rested in my hand. I wanted to believe the hardest part was over, but somehow, I knew. I knew the month I had spent in the hospital was going to be the easy part. No one, absolutely no one could have predicted what was to follow.

A hospital chaplain met us at our son's bedside shortly after I arrived. "Do you wish to baptize him?" asked the kind-looking, brown-haired woman. I could tell that she would have an amazing smile under different circumstances.

"They think he is going to die" was my first thought. Something was very wrong, I just knew. Fully believing our loving God would not condemn a sinless, innocent child, Mike and I dedicated our son to God as we had done with our daughter, Heather. Chaplain Abby poured a few drops of water from a small, white shell over his forehead and prayed. Our little boy would one day have to make his own decision whether or not he would follow God. We, as his parents, can only promise to teach, love, and pray that someday he'd choose to ask Jesus into his heart. Our little one, newly dedicated, was quickly taken for another test.

We were led to a small private conference room in the NICU. With fatigue and shock consuming me, I laid my weakened body on a small couch, closed my eyes, and prayed. Sometime later, a sea of light-blue scrubs entered the small room. Men wearing surgical hats, people we had never met before that moment, began to speak.

"No one would have ever predicted this. It is the gravest form of a connection between the trachea and esophagus. Instead of two tubes, your son has one common tube for both his airway and esophagus. It is very rare—and you need to know that there was nothing you did that caused this. It is not genetic. It is a developmental fluke." Looking directly at both Mike and me, the doctor continued, "You have a choice to make. You can do nothing, and he will surely die. Or, you can allow us to try a surgery that we have never done before, and, even then, he will most likely die. If he does survive, he will need a tracheostomy to keep his airway open, a feeding tube for nutrition, and a long-term IV for medications."

Nothing could have prepared me for these shocking words. Numbness flowed through my entire body, yet inside my brain was screaming. Strange thoughts filled my mind. If he survives, this will be the end of my marriage. I knew many marriages end in divorce when a child dies, has health issues, or special needs. Mike truly valued his free time. A child with a trach and feeding tube—that would change everything. Back in college, I had worked at a camp for kids with all kinds of special needs. Their exhausted moms brought them to camp alone. Most were single parents. Was that going to be me? Would our son ever go to school? Get married? Have children? The whirlwind storm came to a halt at the quietest, strangest thought: "Maybe one day he will be able to color."

The doctor said he was sorry to be so straightforward, but it was the truth. "What would you do if he were your child?" I asked this man I had just met.

"I would give him a chance, but know this, no one will judge you whatever you decide. We are so sorry," answered Dr. Sidman. With that, the medical people and family members exited the room. Mike and I were alone. Mike hugged me tighter than I had ever been held in my entire life. We sobbed, loudly, alone, together. Looking into my eyes, his determined voice, cracking between sobs, said over and over, "No matter what, we will be okay. No matter what, WE…WILL…BE…OKAY!"

We did not have much time to decide. I looked to Mike, my voice gone. "Please give him a chance," my husband told the surgeons. We went back into the NICU to see our boy, perhaps for the last time. Rolls of white gauze running the entire length of his throat were held in place by two strips of thick royal-blue tape. It was an attempt to isolate his airway and protect it from corrosive stomach acid. A ventilator entered his nostril to breathe for him. Heather, his big sister, came to see him. We all prayed together. I held his tiny hand. His face looked angelic. The woman in charge spoke softly to his nurse, "Take as many Polaroids as you can." One of Nurse B's jobs that day was to ensure our infant had a carotid pulse, the artery that brings blood to the brain. She managed to squeeze off a few photos between frequent assessments.

"They do not think he is going to make it," I thought as the camera buzzed, producing a fresh image of a baby in the NICU— my baby, complete with a chin dimple and soft, curly hair.

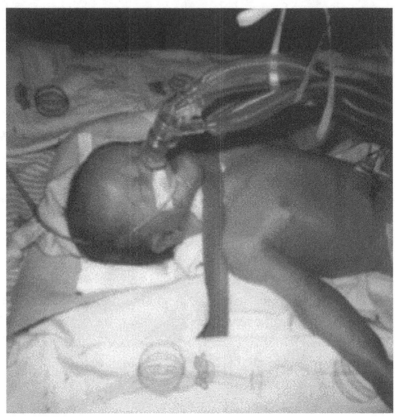

Markus pre-op NICU (May 26, 1999)

CHAPTER 3
Mom: Surgery on Our Newborn

A labor and delivery nurse came to the NICU to check on me. "Why?" I thought. "Oh yeah, I had just given birth, and that is their job." The intense contractions and pushing of labor had already vanished from my mind. The nurse encouraged us to return to the hospital floor I had stayed on for the last thirty days because the surgery would take a long time.

So many people came to the hospital the day Markus was born. I was numb, beyond exhausted, in disbelief that this was all really happening. Most of our family, some friends, our deacon and his wife, along with our interim pastor, even Padre, the minister that had married Mike and me nine years ago, stood with us, waiting.

Heather approached my hospital bed with a beaded-owl keychain kit. "Mommy, will you help me with this?" she asked in her sweet four-year-old voice. The month I had laid in this very bed, I desired nothing more than to be Heather's mommy, to brush her hair, make her a sandwich, to tuck her in at night. Tremors remained in my hands, and my eyes could not focus or comprehend the simple written directions. My shaky fingers struggled to pick up a colorful round bead.

"Heather, let me help you with that," her Aunt Denise, my sister, compassionately offered.

"Thank you," I whispered as she led my precious firstborn out to the lobby. This moment made it clear to me that I was not yet able, physically or mentally, to resume my mommy duties.

Miss Jean, an older woman from a southern state who attended our church, walked in. Openly admitting her directionally challenged ways, Miss Jean explained in her usual southern drawl, "I did not know my way here, but I knew I needed to come." By profession, Miss Jean is a registered nurse. By character, she is one of the sweetest, most genuinely caring individuals I have ever met. "God told me I needed to come," she hugged me tightly. "We need to pray—and now!"

As I lay in that hospital bed, people from church stood in a circle, all of us holding hands and bowing our heads. Miss Jean prayed, bold prayers unlike any I had ever heard before. "Lord, you say it is okay to ask, and I am asking. Lord, we want to see Markus grow up," she stomped her foot as she pleaded. "Lord, we want to play with him. Please." Another foot stomp.

The atrophied muscles in my back regained strength with each word. Yes, yes. From that moment on, my silent prayer was, "Please." I had no other words but "Please" to say over and over.

Three in the morning the phone in my hospital room rang for the fourth time in twelve hours. The operating room nurse reported our son was being taken back to the NICU. He was alive.

Mike and I slept a few hours before heading back to the adjoining Children's Hospital. My vision focused better despite all the puffiness from crying, but my mind could not comprehend all that my eyes were seeing. An infant, our baby, was completely surrounded by machines. He was grayish, so swollen everywhere, covered in tubes and stitches. "What have we done?" I asked myself. Sadness crumpled my heart, seeing his body bruised and still. The room was silent except for the whoosh of the ventilator and occasional beeps from machines. His tiny chest rose a bit with the ventilator hiss, but otherwise he was like a statue. "I am so sorry," I whispered in his ear, noticing the fabric that secured the tube in his throat was completely soaked in dried, brown blood.

A camcorder pointed at our boy caught my attention. Mike was videotaping our Markus. Shock and annoyance instantly filled my mind. "What are you doing?" I asked wide-eyed in a quiet voice, trying to hide my irritated tone. Why would we EVER want to remember this? Record this?

The camcorder paused. "This is part of his story. Some day he is going to tell the world," Mike replied calmly, his glistening eyes locked with mine. The taping continued. His dad was right. We needed to remember, even this.

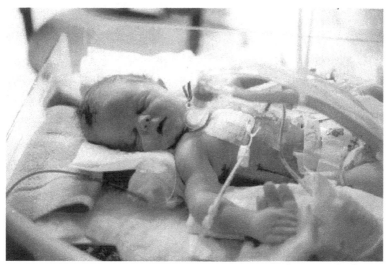

Markus in NICU after surgery

May 27, 1999 (Dad's email)
Later that day, we got to see him for the first time following the surgery. We tried to prepare ourselves again, as we had been trying to prepare ourselves for the last four weeks. It was very good to see him again, but it hurt. His skin

tone was very gray, and he was very puffy. During the surgery, they filled him with fluids and with blood products. His little body was badly swollen from top of his head to the bottom of his feet. All of his bruising, incisions, stitches, etc., were very fresh. More heartache to see your child go through this. We stayed with him for several hours and just looked at him.

The nurse explained what each tube and patch and monitor and machine was. All we could do was to be by his side, talk and sing to him, and stroke his head and arms. I'm not able to explain what the pain is like, to see your child going through something like this, not knowing if he will live, not being able to hold him, or look in his eyes. There is no interaction at all because he is being paralyzed with medicine to keep him from disturbing any of the sutures, inside or out. He is getting morphine and another drug similar to valium, alternately, for pain. He has three kinds of antibiotics flowing into him. He has the trach tube that is hooked up to a respirator. He has a gastro tube that is keeping his esophagus and stomach empty. He has the feeding tube in his belly. He has two tubes draining his chest cavity. He has a catheter. He is on medication to help his kidneys process urine. He has an IV in his umbilical cord, which is where the nurses draw blood for testing. He has sensors stuck on his shoulders and thighs to monitor pulse, blood pressure, and respiration.

He was in really rough shape, and no matter how we thought we had prepared, this was a shock.

CHAPTER 4
Mom: Leaving the Hospital Without Our Son

We requested my discharge orders from the hospital later that same day. I needed to be somewhere we could be alone, somewhere it felt safe to scream. After staring at peach-colored hospital walls for a month, the now-vibrant green trees and bright blue sky overwhelmed, almost burned, my eyes.

Our small house was so quiet. We mostly slept. Mike showed me an internet medical article about laryngotracheoesophageal cleft type IV. "97 percent mortality rate." What? What? I could not even begin to process what I had read.

"He will be the one in twenty. He will be the one in that 3 percent," Mike said as we cried. "He will be the one." His arms wrapped around my shoulders as we sat on the edge of our bed in our very silent house.

Mike called the hospital frequently that first day and night, each time hearing that our son was stable, *we let out a breath we did not even realize we were holding*. We slept, cried, and prayed. In the morning, I got up to use the breast pump my family had given me as a gift. I tried to read the directions in order to put it together. It should have been simple—and truly it probably was—but I could not follow the instructions. I completely broke down, sobbing loudly. "Do I even bother trying to do this?" I thought, feeling completely helpless. My pained sobs woke up Mike.

"I can't figure this out. I can't figure this out," I cried, utterly defeated.

Mike blinked hard. "It's okay. We will do this together. This is one of the first things we are going to figure out together." His hands held my slumped, overwhelmed shoulders, "No matter what."

We visited Markus again in the hospital before driving over to stay with Heather at my parents' house. We needed help. At their house, we could leave at a moment's notice, and Heather would be safe with her grandparents. It was so wonderful to hug Heather while standing up. Her excitement was evident from the tight squeeze she gave me and the giant smile on her face. Mike quietly picked up my mom's Wheel of Fortune handheld video game. "Really?" I thought. "How can you do that right now with everything going on?" Knowing we all process grief and difficulties differently, I chalked it up to that even though I found it slightly strange. The electronic click of the spinning wheel occasionally floated from the living room to my parents' kitchen.

"Deb," Mike said, walking slowly towards me, his eyes wide with guarded surprise. "Look at this first puzzle I did. The category was 'event.'" He stared in shock at the Wheel of Fortune video game screen. Bending to look over his shoulder, I saw the answer that had stopped Mike so completely: M-I-R-A-C-L-E.

I sat down next to him, my eyes fixed on that one word: *miracle*.

CHAPTER 5

Mom: The NICU Emotional Rollercoaster

ike needed to return to work. Cell phones were not all the rage in 1999, but I was very grateful that Mike now carried one. Each day seemed so long and full of both good news and heaviness. We clung to those positive reports when it felt like the downhill section of this roller coaster ride was too steep and scary.

Heather often came along to visit Markus at Children's. The hospital has what is called the "sibling play area." Child life specialists and volunteers provide a safe, fun place for siblings to spend ninety minutes, allowing parents one-on-one time with their hospitalized child. My daughter especially liked the crafts, games, and fancy outdoor teeter-totter during her short stays. I settled her into the sibling play area before heading back to hold Markus.

I pushed the cushioned glider rocker next to my baby's bedside. The nurse lifted him and carefully placed him in my arms. Numerous tubes and lines were cautiously arranged. I breathed deep, looking into his eyes. He looked right back. My smile widened. "Markus, look at you, sweet boy," I whispered. Everything seemed fine, then all of a sudden, his little body squirmed, his nose and eyes crinkled as though he might cry, but instead, he stopped breathing. In seconds, my infant's cheeks quickly turned white and lips became blue as his eyes rolled back in their sockets.

His entire body went limp. Loud alarms screeched. Two nurses quickly placed his lifeless body back in the bed. An ambu bag was attached to his trach tube. Oxygen squeezed from the inflated bag caused his tiny chest to rise. The second nurse used two fingers to do compressions on his breastbone. The thought, "He just died in my arms," raced through my mind as I stood by watching. "Four weeks—and he just died. Is this how it ends?"

Medical people rushed to his bed. The monitors had quieted. His chest was again moving with the ventilator. Dr. Sidman came and looked in his airway with a thin scope. The sutures had not been damaged, and the trach tube looked fine and unobstructed. I overheard Dr. Sidman tell the nurse, "Be sure to get him back in Mom's arms as soon as possible." I was shocked and stunned because Markus had changed so quickly right in my arms. Mike came immediately after I called. Relief flooded my mind, realizing Heather had not witnessed one second of the episode, and that our son was still alive.

Dr. Sidman explained that a normal airway is rigid, but Markus's was floppy. The soft tissue in his trachea had closed off his airway. He referred to it as a spell, more specifically, a "dying spell."

"I am so sorry this happened while you were holding him," said Dr. Sidman. "I assure you it was not the result of anything you did, nor could you have prevented it. Unfortunately, it will happen again"—terrifying words to hear, but true. It did happen again. Fortunately, squeezing the ambu bag hooked up to his trach tube or quickly changing the trach tube reopened his airway during repeat episodes. Hopefully, with time, Markus's tissue in his trachea would firm up, and these horrible episodes would end. Until then, expecting that it would happen again sometimes made it hard for me to breathe, let alone think straight.

In the NICU, we had days in which it seemed like our child was not going to survive, and then other days we would walk into absolute, unexpected surprises. Two weeks later, I entered the dimly lit room to see my son sitting in a blue baby seat looking at a colorful mobile hanging above him. Not only that, but he now was in a crib and he was *wearing actual baby clothes.* What? Nurse T said matter-of-factly, "Let's see what this boy can do." Seeing him in something so normal like an infant seat was both exciting and terrifying. She told me that the v-neck snap-up onesies work really well for babies with lots of tubes. My gaze remained riveted. My son was sitting in an infant seat. My son was wearing baby clothes.

On my way home I had to make a stop to shop. In the baby section, I found six v-neck snap-up onesies, all in different patterns: light-blue baseballs, muted-green zoo animals, vibrant dinosaurs. They looked adorable and felt so soft. I placed one of each style, size three months, in the shopping cart. I froze, seeing the same exact outfits in the six-month size. "Do I dare? Will he live to ever wear these?" An entire conversation took place in my head as I studied those larger sizes for a good ten minutes, while shaking, crying, and staring. Suddenly, those strong, inspiring words spoken by Nurse T repeated themselves over and over, *"Let's see what this boy can do."* Into the cart went six of the larger sizes as well. My baby was still in the NICU, but from now on he would wear baby clothes. In my mind, he just took a giant leap forward.

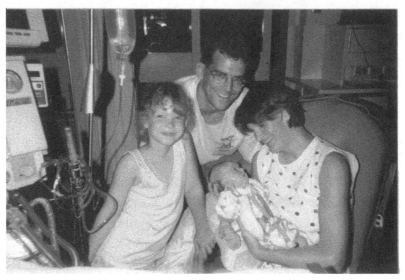

First family photo with Markus in NICU (1999)

CHAPTER 6
Mom: Homecoming

Markus was heavy. For over five months, I had not carried him farther than four feet from his bed. Plastic blue tubing attached to his throat, the feeding tube connected to the IV pole, and the cord taped to his toe to measure oxygen allowed him only a four-foot leash. November 2, 1999, would be different. Today we would leave the hospital with our son—five months and one week after he was born. Cradling Markus in my right arm and pulling an oxygen tank with my left, I was determined that I would carry him out the door. I felt like there should be fanfare as we began leaving or, at the minimum, police officers blocking the hospital hallways. Because really, *how could we do this at home?* I mean, we had taken the trach classes, CPR, learned feeding tubes and long-term IV care, the necessary skills, but now we were stepping into the unknown. Our medically fragile child was coming to our house; he was coming home.

No one stopped us. Truly, no one really seemed to take notice at all. Home we drove, an infant in the back seat hooked up to a feeding pump, oxygen tank, and a pulse oximeter. His arms sprawled to the side in a heavy navy-blue snowsuit. His eyes scanned everywhere. A homecare nurse sat next to him.

We celebrated his homecoming that week by doing the craziest thing—we watched a cartoon video in our living room. Markus laid on the floor, his head and shoulders elevated on a semi-circular pillow. Heather was right next to him with her head on a pillow. The homecare nurse stayed in Markus's bedroom for a short while. It was the first time the four of us, our family, had ever been alone. *And it was nothing short of incredible.*

CHAPTER 7
Mom: If He Makes It to One...

The months after bringing Markus home were filled with great joy as well as new and terrifying territory. What do we do when Markus cries in pain as yellow stomach fluid, more specifically, stomach acid, gushes out the hole in his tummy, burning delicate skin as it travels across his abdomen before puddling on the floor? Dr. Kennedy recommended draining his stomach feeding tube into a diaper. It worked. The rivers of acid now poured into the diaper instead of down his belly.

I still had so many questions.

How do I *not show my fear* as a bluish, eerie tinge spreads over his lips and face from his crying?

Would the trach tube in his neck get plugged with thick mucus?

Would his airway collapse, causing another "dying spell"? Staff in the NICU called it that. He would struggle for a few seconds, stop breathing, lose consciousness, turn blue, and then his heart rate would crash. We kept an ambu bag and oxygen tank next to him for years to force air into his lungs when this happened.

Or on the flip side, what do I do differently when he gets something more normal, like a fever? His care was so night-and-day different from raising my first child.

Heather had infrequent wheezing, but only if she was battling an upper respiratory illness. With Markus, every day it was about attempting to prevent illness or dealing with the fallout from the latest "illness bug" gone crazy. The day Markus made it to his first birthday, Mike and I realized we needed in-depth, legit medical knowledge. How could we best help our son? Our solution was for me to study nursing. It was a good fit for my undergraduate degree in community health and athletic training. One class at a time, and four years later, I could legally sign my name as Debra Bachman, registered nurse.

The medical information that I acquired on my registered nurse path was incredibly valuable, even the chemistry. I looked at things so differently, surprised that I could understand processes from this new viewpoint. During my first semester of college as an "older" adult, I found the answer to my fever question. An increase in body temperature speeds up numerous body processes. If reactions are occurring at a faster rate, then more oxygen is needed. Plain and simple, Markus's body could not keep up with the increased oxygen demands brought on by a fever. Fever-reducing medications and additional oxygen from a tank were necessary to support his little body. Going back to school involved sacrifice for our family. Pursuing a nursing degree turned out to be an invaluable investment with immeasurable benefits.

Markus busy playing at home (August 2000)

CHAPTER 8
Mom: "He May Not Talk..."

Tests given him as an infant indicated Markus had some hearing loss. Though important, this bonus issue, as we call it, took a huge back seat when compared to the breathing and eating challenges that dictated our days. Thankfully, I had taken two courses in American Sign Language (ASL) in college. This second language became valuable not only in my career but also more importantly, for my son. Amazingly enough, Markus learned to make sounds and then words, despite the trach tube in his airway. By tilting his head to the side and pointing his chin down, he could force air up through his vocal cords to coo and babble. At the same time, his hands became proficient communicators. I can still see the absolute sparkling joy in his eyes as he signed the words "balloon" or "outside." His little voice was hard to understand, but he had learned and was continuing to learn how to talk.

Early childhood teachers encouraged Markus to point at pictures to help him communicate, but he had no interest in those photos. Signing was his preference—that is until the day he wore his first hearing aid. The magic of this new discovery called "clearer sound" shone on his face. From that day on, this little man was adamant, practically dramatic.

"No sign, Mama! No sign!" his high-pitched, gurgling voice insisted.

"We can still do both, Markus," I tried to reason.

Loose curls bounced side to side, his head shaking back and forth while his little hands covered both eyes.

I was not going to win this one. Gratefully, the language groundwork had been laid. He was determined to master speaking and listening with his new hearing aid. ASL is still quite handy for us in a crowd, across a noisy room, or when Markus is unable to speak with his mouth. Much of his valuable ASL skills have been forgotten, but, thankfully, some words are still locked in his memory. Two of my personal favorites are "stop" and "wait," very practical parent words that he knows well.

Heather and Markus having fun getting wet!

CHAPTER 9
Markus: Life as I Know It

My parents insist it is a gift that I do not dwell on difficulties.

Tragedy and pain are actually a very normal part of life.

I find that the stretches between those critical moments contain absolute treasures, if I intentionally seek them.

Now in 2016, at the age of 17, I struggle to comprehend these stories and events that make up my beginning. I read old emails and articles written about me, look at old pictures, and yet, it is almost surreal to believe they are all centered around . . . me. I have heard many stories from friends, relatives, and even some neighbors, but it is all a blank. In old photos, my smile is often enormous, looking as if my mouth had reached its maximum stretch capacity. Or, maybe somehow, that is what I see because I am able to look past all the tubes. *Not everyone can do that.* I do recall, thankfully, lots of happy moments from some of my younger days; most with such intense joy that, to this day, I smile replaying them like short movies in my mind. Those are the types of memories that I choose to dwell on when my mind wanders back in time. I have my definite favorites, like every one of our summer vacations up north.

Each July, my family, along with all of Mom's side, rents a bunch of cabins in the tiny town of Villard, Minnesota. It is always my favorite week of the year, packed with adventure and lots of time together. For many years, I could not swim or go water tubing behind the speedboat with my cousins because of the hole in my neck called a tracheostomy. My alternative activity, which I loved so, so much, was serving as the all-time spotter for whoever was driving the boat. It was my important duty to let the driver know when someone got dumped into the lake. Some of my older cousins' wipeouts made me laugh like crazy. They are a most entertaining, lovable bunch. Occasionally, I was also allowed to steer the speedboat with my uncles. Those Minnesota lakes looked huge as an ocean through my young eyes. However, when I saw a real ocean, I realized that most Minnesota lakes look like puddles in comparison.

In August 2005, when I was six, I was granted a Make-A-Wish trip to meet a killer whale. I guess I was over-the-top nutso about marine animals at the time. I got to fly in an actual airplane over the Rocky Mountains and saw the tall tip-tops of them. While in San Diego, California, Mom, Dad, Heather, and I went to Sea World to meet a live killer whale named Ulysses Shamu. I would think anyone would permanently retain memory of every second spent petting, hugging, and feeding a 10,000-pound ocean creature or being allowed to give him various commands, but I do not. My sister kissed Ulysses Shamu. Mom told him thank you. I have seen pictures and heard the stories, but I have no recollection of Sea World. However, our scrapbook tells the amazing once-in-a-lifetime story of a six-year-old me on one exceptionally joyful California adventure. Somehow, my parents recall every moment.

Markus, 6, and Heather, 11, feeding giraffes at the San Diego
Zoo (2005)

During our trip we also visited the San Diego Zoo. What
clearly sticks out, and I can visualize them even now, is standing
next to the giraffes. Those long-necked beauties leisurely came up
to the fence, and then down came that big, lolling, purple tongue
sticking out at us. I cannot recollect the fancy limousine that picked
us up and brought us home, but I can vividly see that giraffe
"giving us the raspberries."

However oddball the wonderful giraffe encounter was, often
I was not dealt such sweet cards.

Even as a little guy, in all honesty, my health has always been
an all-out war. My chest is covered with what Mom refers to as
battle scars or "tattoos with a story." Hospitalizations became the
norm because I would often get sick with pneumonia or some lung
thing. Every stay was filled with tests, x-rays, IV pokes, and a

handful of mylar balloons. Those floating, colorful creations would be all over the place in my hospital room. A few were always tied to the bedrails, making it convenient for me to fidget and toy with them all day. I'd spend, I don't know, hours curling up the ribbon, admiring the way they formed such perfect, bouncy spirals. Literally, I was fascinated by balloons. My favorite movie, of course, was *The Red Balloon*. In fact, I liked it so much my Uncle Dan would find the largest red one he could get his hands on for me whenever I was admitted for a hospital stay.

I find it surprising how little my brain has held onto. I know I did lots each day, yet I don't truly remember much, or so it seems. It's like I see my life as it happens, yet retaining every moment must not be possible. Maybe there is a maximum capacity in the personal library of my brain, and some stuff has to be thrown out the window to make room for what has yet to come.

Time occasionally seems to crawl by, but I think time, in reality, is zipping past quite rapidly. Parents definitely speak as if it's true. It's like we are born, zoom into grade school, in a flash we're in high school, and so many other things happen all in a short amount of time—if we are lucky. Old age is not a gift we all get to unwrap, that's what my Aunt Denise says. We are not all guaranteed the same number of breaths in this life. This makes me extra grateful that not all of my early childhood memories were permanently deleted from my memory bank.

My sister, Heather, was a Girl Scout. Every year she would call people and also hike around the whole neighborhood, filling up her sheet with Girl Scout cookie orders. Her sales were often huge, probably around two to three hundred boxes of Thin Mints, Trefoils, Do-Si-Dos, and whatever the new flavor was that year. To me, separating the inventory according to customer was the best game we ever played. Her bedroom became a rainbow of boxes strewn all over the floor and bed, almost like dynamite had left colorful rubble everywhere. I say this because we have a small house, and I was definitely shorter back then. It was a beautiful mess of a puzzle for us to figure out.

We worked well together, Heather and I. Rarely did we disagree, but it did happen. On our killer whale trip to San Diego, our parents told us that Mom was pregnant. I was ecstatic, but Heather . . . not so much. "Well, it better be a girl!" she said with a bossy, bratty tone. I am sure she was nervous about the possibility of another sibling that required extensive medical attention, but that thought never crossed my mind.

At one point, Dad had written in an email: *"Now our normal includes things like feeding tubes, trachs, barely audible raspy sounds, and visits that end in leaving our baby behind. These are all things that Heather now views as normal, too, which is really messed up"* (October 18, 1999).

Nothing but pure excitement raced through me at the thought of passing on the title of the youngest in the family. My dear 11-year-old sister quickly changed her tune the day Noah was born in 2006. And me, at six-and-a-half, became and continue to be one proud big brother.

During those cookie business days, we had a steady stream of day and night nurses to help take care of me. Sweetly enough, the nurses were also some of Heather's loyal customers. However, that part of life, the homecare agency nursing, is mostly lost to me. Old photos and writings tell the story of how much help Mom and Dad certainly needed in order to raise me at home with such health problems. Realistically, my situation was too much for any parent to handle alone on a daily basis. Mom and Dad would have crashed and burned if it wasn't for the nurses and others that stepped in. It is so humbling to think they were completely immersed in our family life because of me. Wish I could thank them all now.

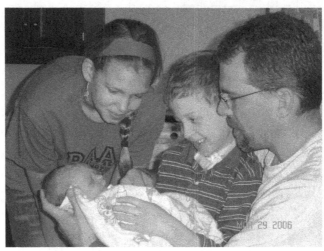

Welcoming baby Noah (2006)

Heather, Markus, and Noah at Christmas (2006)

CHAPTER 10
Markus: When the Hospital is a Second Home

L ife has not always been easy for me. For seventeen years, my health seems to ride a certain wave or pattern throughout the year. During the spring and summer months, I am typically healthy and active. I jump at every opportunity to try new things as well as those things I already enjoy. When the start of school comes around in September, I am doing well and am in school for the fall. However, once December rolls around, my health seems to fall into a valley. Sometimes the valleys are shallow, and I bounce back quickly; other times they're deep and quite rocky. In those hard places, recovery has been very, very slow.

Since I was a baby in the NICU, I have struggled with pneumonia and MRSA (methicillin-resistant staphylococcus aureus). They both like to show up around December 25 like an unwanted, recycled Christmas gift. My heart rate shoots up way too high, and then my oxygen numbers dangerously drop. Pain radiates throughout my chest, usually right in the area the invader has tried to overtake. Mile-high fever rages within, causing such weakness that I need help to walk the fifteen feet from my bed to the bathroom. Next thing we know, I am driven to Children's Minnesota Hospital to get admitted. IV meds, a barrage of tests, chest x-rays, blood draws, so . . . many . . . blood draws until I am wheeled into a hospital room. This becomes my "private apartment" for at least a week, usually longer. The numerous medical people dressed in their color-coded scrubs, like friendly neighbors, knock before they come in to see me each day.

I feel so miserable when I need to go to the hospital—both physically and emotionally. Physically, I endure some nasty sickness. Emotionally, I feel like I mess up the family dynamics and add so much stress on everyone. I hate being the reason my family gets separated. Hate it, and yet I am most grateful that one of my parents usually stays there with me. It is truly impossible for me to keep track of all my health care needs and to communicate clearly when I am feeling so lousy. The first few days I am not able to do much besides watch television, sleep, and maybe read. We don't have cable TV at home, so a big treat for me is watching Animal Planet and the Food Network. I spend hours watching those two channels, and maybe occasionally watch something else if I am lucky enough that it catches my eyes and interest. As my condition improves, I might start to play cards or maybe some video games.

Coming from a person who relies totally on a feeding tube, Food Network probably sounds like a weird obsession. However, I used to be able to eat a little, mostly before I got my trach out. After my windpipe was enclosed, it became extremely hard for me to safely coordinate chewing, breathing, and swallowing. I also realized that throwing up was one of my *very least favorite activities*. Vomiting commonly followed my attempt to eat by mouth, which can be a pretty strong deterrent. My ultimate culinary choice was probably tiny slices of hot cheese pizza—or was it a birthday cake with thick, creamy frosting? Honestly, it all sounds pretty dreamy to me now, but not the puking part.

Episodes of "Chopped" are a primo distraction during my hospital stays. Contestants work with an unknown basket of ingredients that must be incorporated into a dish of their choice.

Of course, it has to be completed within a ridiculously short amount of time. This may sound cruel, but my favorite episode ever had habanero pepper as one of the mystery ingredients. A petite female chef had supposedly never heard of them. She cut off a piece and very matter-of-factly chewed it up. "Not bad," the black-haired woman said calmly. She then used that extremely hot pepper *as a vegetable in a stir-fry*. OH, MAN! Picturing the judges' faces as they tasted her dish makes me giggle even today. Imagine their poor mouths as they reached for water and wiped the sweat from their foreheads! I cannot even slightly fathom the intense heat because once I dipped my finger in BBQ sauce, and it lit my tongue on fire. My parents insist that it was a super-mild honey BBQ sauce, which I hear is totally not hot, but to me, it burned. I know, I'm wimpy, which is why I should not even chuckle at those judges' misery, and yet I must confess, I belly laugh every time I watch it.

Thankfully, the hospital staff has been good at keeping my brain engaged during my many stays. Children's Minnesota has an incredible department called Child Life. The child life specialists help both the patient and their siblings understand what is happening and offer some helpful ways to cope. These hospital professionals also bring fun things to do, like puzzles, games, art supplies, movies, almost anything a kid could dream of, including arranging visits from therapy animals. These distractions are an absolute sanity saver and an essential piece of the healing journey.

Children's Minnesota has its own television channel that they stream throughout the hospital. They do all kinds of programs on that station, and they have something new every day for patients. One day, it could be a game show, where you can call in to share your answers with the host. The main character, in my opinion, is The Dude. He is an awesome guy. Total clown, totally chill, and he can make you laugh without even trying. The two of us have known each other for quite a while now. Whenever I call in, even if it has been a while since my last stay, he seems to recognize my voice, which I find quite cool. Bingo days are my favorite. Patients know when it was one of those days because the red-vested volunteers stop in with a stack of preprinted cards along with a flyer. Bingo is definitely a "go" during my hospital stays.

I have never been very lonely in the hospital, as I have lots of visitors once I am stable and strong enough to chat, which was great fun for me. Sometimes I knew who was coming, and other times it was a surprise. Many days, it was not uncommon to have various family and friends visit with me. In fact, occasionally I was dubbed "Mr. Popular" or something similar by my nurses because I had so many visitors. Not that I don't enjoy all the attention and love, but it felt kind of weird being called "Mr. Popular." It reminded me a little bit of that guy on TV's "Shark Tank" they call Mr. Wonderful. His nickname is, I believe, in jest, and mine was well, weird. I am happy and content to be me.

In the hospital, two things made me have terrible panic attacks: IVs and the Operating Room (OR). As a young kid, I eventually figured out that every time that huge, clunky IV cart rolled into the room, I was looking at more needle injection attempts. My mind and emotions would start doing cartwheels, and next thing my parents know, I would be bawling up a storm and breathing fast—and they had not even started the process of accessing an IV! It was a struggle to get me to relax enough for the vein to get accessed, and, at times, they could not get one in on the first try because I would be so tensed up. My intensity would not subside until after they had taped up my arm and secured the IV. Thing is, after being a repeat patient and needing so many IVs, eventually my arms and hands could no longer support having them. It got so bad that the veins would not even last twenty-four hours before collapsing, getting too inflamed or bursting.

We had to find a better solution, and we did in the fall of 2009: a port-a-cath. However, in order for this to happen, I would have to deal with my other huge fear, the OR.

I dread the OR even more than those IV needle sticks. Thankfully I have no idea when this all started, but nonetheless, going back to the OR would trigger anxiety in me. I can still see those bright, bright lights and lots of stainless steel, but the one thing that got me feeling nauseated every time was the smell in that room. It sure was not a pleasant smell to me, and my stomach felt like a pile of soup. I would cry, scream, maybe even get nauseated and vomit. You would not think I would have enough time to do all of that, but I somehow managed. Mom and Dad would both come back with me. They would talk to me and squeeze my hands until I was knocked out by the drugs. Then all of a sudden, I was waking up in the recovery room, and Mom and Dad would be there with their groggy son waking from a not-so-pleasant slumber. As I got older, I realized I had to get a grip and control the anxiety and panic in healthy ways, not allowing fear to overtake me.

It took me quite a while to figure out how to control the episodes of panic, but thankfully, I have found ways that work for IV sticks and the OR. For IVs, I do a couple of things. Turning my head so I cannot see what is going on is one. This helps because seeing the needle triggers these episodes. If it is an option, I will also request that numbing cream be applied to help lessen the pain from the needle. Sometimes it is so effective I do not feel the needle whatsoever, and, when I look, it is already done! In addition to these two things, if I am able to, I also play contemporary Christian music. This helps me mentally by focusing on something other than that incoming needle and pain I know all too well. The music also calms my spirit. For blood draws, I usually request my favorite lab guy, Mr. Claude, if he is available. His confident, relaxed presence is not only a great distraction, but, more importantly, he somehow finds my veins on the first try. He is an ace. I do not know how Mr. Claude does it, but he totally has a great talent, and it is a good day for me when he is working. Nurses from the infusion team are also super good at placing IV lines when I need them. These distractions do not take away the entire discomfort, but they have truly helped me get a grip on my consuming sense of hysteria. Thankfully it rarely happens anymore. My methods for dealing with my fears of the OR are a little different, but they are as effective in their own ways.

Ask people what their least favorite place is in a hospital, I could probably just about guarantee that at least half, if not more, would say the operating room. It is definitely my least favorite place and a major source of intense alarm that rushes through my brain. Now that I am older, though, I determined that it was time to figure a way out to deal with this stressor. After some experimenting, a method was found, and I have stuck to it. In reality, you are not awake for long when you get back to the OR, and your eyes are starting to shut as you fall into a medicated, deep slumber. Knowing this, I do not even bother to open my eyes as soon as I am headed for that dreaded, ever-so-brightly lit room. Even though I am no longer a little kid, I ask to be rolled back to the OR on a gurney, so I do not have to walk and see where I am going. Also, my hearing is pretty lousy. I am completely deaf in my right ear and use a hearing aid in my left. To quiet any noises that could lead to dismay, I remove the hearing aid prior to leaving the pre-op area. Since I choose not to see or hear where I am, I listen closely to instruction and my parents. My eyes remain glued shut until I wake up in the recovery room. It works every time.

I know some people would probably feel stressed by not seeing what is going on, but, for me, I cannot watch, because I will start spinning out of control. Another thing I do that helps is when the doctors and anesthesiologist come and talk with me prior to the surgery, I explain to them that the OR is a huge stressor for me. In order for me to deal with it, I request that once they get me back there, they knock me out as quickly as possible. They have been most helpful and accommodating, referring to me as one *with the privileges of a seasoned frequent flyer.* However, one time I was given the knockout drug too fast, and I felt a burning in my chest before falling asleep. I uttered the word "Oowwww" before I was out. After that experience, I now request to do it quickly, but not too fast, because nobody enjoys a fiery sensation in their chest.

Doing all these things has helped me manage my episodes in the OR, and, seriously, this strategy has been a life changer. I do not like the OR, and that will probably never change. Nonetheless, I have found ways to manage my negative feelings and fears, and I will keep using them as long as I have to because, dang it, *I know they work.*

CHAPTER II
Markus: Learning With a Twist

School is something everyone does. It's normal, regular, and expected. It is the place for learning the basics needed to become working men and women. School is one thing I thoroughly enjoy. I thrive on the challenge of learning new things, stretching my cerebral comfort zone, and investigating the unknown.

Public school worked out quite well for me. Despite my challenges, I attended when my health permitted. Crazy as it sounds, my all-time favorite part of those elementary years was a timed math test. The ultimate goal was to correctly answer as many math problems as possible. I found the famous "Hot Pencil Test" to be a well-thought-out progression through addition, subtraction, multiplication, division, and finally all of them combined on one magical test. I thoroughly enjoyed the occasional madness that would seem to float around, everyone hunched over their test, furiously writing down answers in the few precious minutes we were given. I flew through pretty much all of them, and I felt so lucky to experience the privilege of attempting the hardest tests. It was the fastest I ever moved. My lungs may have prevented my ability to be a sprinter, but they could not stop me from my favorite personal racetrack, a.k.a. math.

Most days there was no way I could go outside to play at recess. Either the Minnesota weather was too cold for my lungs, or I had to do breathing treatments. Sometimes classmates would take turns keeping me company inside. We would play games or get to use the class computer. Otherwise, it was only the nurse and me. In fifth grade, I was an office helper during recess. Stapling papers and chatting with the adults worked well for me. Truth be told, I loved it.

What a change it was moving from Normandale Hills Elementary to Olson Middle School in the sixth grade. Gone were the days of one main teacher and one classroom. I physically had to adjust to walking from class to class within three minutes, *no ifs, ands, or buts.* Being late was not acceptable and resulted in earning a dreaded tardy, even if you were only one minute past the bell. Thing was, I had an exception written into my "Individualized Education Plan" (IEP) that I could be late without being counted as tardy. However, that was not part of my character. Being late bugged me. And why should I be treated differently just because my breathing was an issue?

In middle school, the piles of homework suddenly became a little higher as I juggled seven classes. I realized that time management was even more important than when I was in fifth grade. It helped me prioritize things, and I saw the real value of my beloved planner. Everything could be logically written down. I appreciate *logical.* It was tricky for me at first, but I eventually got the hang of it. The habits I made then have stuck with me. One such habit is shoving all my leisure interests aside until I complete every assignment that needs my immediate attention, including studying for upcoming tests. It's good to know that truly valuable skills can be learned in middle school.

In sixth grade, my science teacher, Mrs. S, would occasionally bring her dog to school, and oh, *did we go crazy over her dog.* That black, brown, and white fluffy guy loved attention. One cool thing about this dog was that he was blind. It wasn't every day I met such a great dog that also happened to have a disability. We students would all huddle around him, giving him a good petting until we were ordered to our own seats so the lesson could begin. I must admit, some days it wasn't always so easy to focus on the lesson when that loveable dog was in the room, but I somehow managed.

For eighth grade Family and Consumer Science (FACS), I had to do a volunteer project. This was an easy one for me. I decided to make some large fleece tie blankets for kids at Children's Minnesota. I knew full well that the thin, white hospital blankets provided to patients are not the most comfortable. From what I had seen, donated tie blankets are often sized for little kids, but not for teenagers. Making the cozy, colorful gifts for older kids was a most fun and unusual assignment. Surprisingly, I also found myself feeling pretty good inside. This whole experience solidified what's so true: Helping others truly benefits the giver as well, and it was only a few blankets.

A short time after I had handed in my report on my volunteer project, I received a letter from Olson Middle School saying that my FACS teacher had chosen me for a "student of the trimester" award. I did not see that coming, and when I learned why she nominated me, I was surprised. It had to do with that volunteer project. I had done what I was supposed to do without expecting anything except a grade, nothing else. This was a real honor and highlight of my Olson days. Middle school may not be a common favorite for some, but I loved those three short years. My health was far from perfect, but life continued happening all around me, and I was determined not to miss anything.

CHAPTER 12
Markus: Outdoor Adventures Are Calling

Uncle Dan helping Markus cross a river on a hunting trip (2012)

Okay, this might sound ironic to some when I say I am both an animal lover and a hunter. However, I think it is something that runs in my family. Papa, my uncles, and several cousins all hunt, so I think I got the "bug" from Mom's side of the family. During middle school, I first exhibited an interest in hunting. I was recovering from pneumonia in the hospital. The head of my hospital bed was raised to an almost sitting posture to help make breathing more comfortable. Mom was going through her emails. She opened one that was an invitation to a turkey hunt sponsored by the United Special

Sportsman Alliance (USSA). Somehow I caught a glimpse of it from my bed.

"I want to do that," I said as I adjusted the nasal cannula.

Mom looked at me kind of shocked. I am not sure if she saw me as someone who would turn into a hunter at all, yet, at that moment, I guess I did. The event was a couple of months off, and I was a total train wreck health-wise at the time of that email. In the hospital, on oxygen and IV meds, coughing up yucky stuff— and I was saying that *I wanted to go*! Mom mulled it over.

"You can go. It's going to require quite a bit of work on your part, but okay," she tentatively said. With that, she signed me up for my first-ever hunt. And gun-safety training, of course, is vital to anyone considering hunting.

Before I knew it, mid-May had rolled around, and that meant turkey time had arrived. The hunt took place in Austin, Minnesota, about fifteen minutes west of Rochester. All the hunters were paired up with a guide for the weekend-long turkey extravaganza.

I was assigned to Mr. Linden. He was a tall man with large, round glasses and thinner gray hair. There was an undeniably kind, gentle, spunky grandparent-like way about him. Mr. Linden took his time explaining the plan for our exact hunting spot as well as the best way to set up in the blind. I could not hold the 20-gauge shotgun in the regular fashion because my implanted IV was exactly where I needed to shoulder the gun. The kick from that firearm could damage my port-a-cath, which would be a disaster. Holding the 20-gauge in a stand was the safest option for me.

"RRIINNGGG!!!!" Four o'clock in the morning and it's pitch-black outside. Mom, Uncle Dan, and I were already up so my uncle and I could be out the door in time to sneakily get to our spot. We wanted to be in place before those giant birds woke up. I was both excited and quite tired, but oh, oh, so ready for this new adventure.

The sun was starting to creep up over the horizon, illuminating a wide-open field. The first rays were shining off the trees that lined the edge of the woods. After hustling for a few minutes, we were settled and started the waiting game. Watching the woods wake up in the morning was absolutely amazing. Bugs, birds, and then the smaller animals started scampering about. A sight like this could never be replicated on even the most spectacular, well-done nature documentary.

Shortly after sunrise, a group of turkeys wandered down the tree line towards the edge of the field. Mr. Linden did a few female turkey calls, attempting to convince this bachelor group to come closer. The toms (the males) needed to ideally be within thirty yards or closer before I would be able to fire a shot. After a few rounds of calling, we kept hush and watched with great anticipation. The turkey group leisurely plodded towards us. Could this really be happening? Breathing became faster and shallower as an unfamiliar type of adrenaline rushed through my body. They waddled closer yet. POOF! Turkey wings and legs were instantly scrambling, and in a matter of a few seconds, they all vanished thanks to one fast, swooping bald eagle. The entire flock frantically ran for safety. From that point on, only a lone female walked right outside our blind. Hens are off-limits in the spring, but she was interesting to watch. We could almost have reached out and touched her. It was such an exciting experience to see all those turkeys and observe their behavior. The whole sight was mesmerizing. After that, I was hooked. I wanted to keep on hunting despite the fact that at times nature decides not to play in your favor.

Special Youth Challenge (SYC) is another group that has allowed me to participate in their hunting events. Both SYC and USSA are volunteer organizations that sponsor fishing and hunting trips for kids with life-threatening conditions. I qualified because of my complicated respiratory system and other health issues. Each weekend was an amazing time with some incredibly fabulous people. Most of the volunteers are hunters who are so much fun to be around. There I have been able to meet and spend time with other kids also facing difficult health-related trials. It is great that none of that seems to matter in those forty-eight weekend hours. Some days I have even been able to bring home wild game. My first such experience of nature playing in my favor came when I went to Wisconsin for my second turkey hunt.

Before I knew it, Mom, Uncle Dan, and I were all piling into the car for yet another hunt. We stayed at a small, simple, single-story old dorm-like place. Inside, there was a gathering and eating area for all the hunters, guides, and families to come together. Bedrooms were located at opposite ends of the building. Each had two walls lined with bunks. The highlight was not the building, but the people and the hunting. This trip, I brought home a large gobbler. It now felt official: *I was actually a hunter.* Camouflage and blaze orange became my new favorite colors.

CHAPTER 13
Markus: An Unfortunate New Direction

What happened in the spring of my eighth-grade year came out of the blue. Yes, I have had health issues, but this was brand new, and it dragged on. Without any warning, at age 14, I started coughing up vibrant, fresh, red blood, and it was often quite a bit. What the heck? The red-tinged sputum alarmed my parents, but for the most part, I felt normal.

We tried to figure out what was causing the bleeding. At first, we suspected it was a new medicine substitute that was producing the unwelcomed irritation and bleeding.

Dad had switched jobs that same spring, and when he did, one of the most expensive respiratory medicines I needed was denied by the new insurance. The insurance company said they would cover something "similar" that should "do the same thing as my current one." From a chemistry standpoint, it sounded like it might work. However, shortly after the switch, my real problems began.

We tried many different things to try and stop what was causing so much lung irritation. First, we cut back on the new nebulized medication. We were hopeful at first, but things did not improve. Then we removed it entirely, but that did not solve the problem either. Mom and Dad kept trying to get my old medicine approved, but the insurance company kept denying it. After they had tried a few times, one of my uncles, who is a lawyer, got involved. Thanks to one letter, there was an immediate call to my lung doctor. The old medicine was quickly approved. There was a notable decrease in blood when this respiratory treatment was once again part of the daily routine, but, unfortunately, the bleeding did not completely stop.

After dragging on for a few months, it almost became normal and expected. I would usually say, "It was a lot," or "It was a little." In addition to the amount, the color would also vary. Some days it was bright red. Other days, it was a darker red or even brown, which means old blood. Neither is ideal, but we were not as worried if it was brown stuff that came out. However, we had no exact idea of what was causing it, and we also did not know for sure if it was coming from my lungs, stomach, or somewhere else. We had ideas, but the exact cause would not be confirmed until December of my freshman year.

Little did we understand how different life was going to be not only for me, but also for my family.

It was time to get more invasive to figure out this puzzle. A trip to the operating room to look in my airway did not reveal the specific cause. The next day, I had an appointment with Dr. Sidman, who had been my ENT (ear, nose, and throat) physician from day one. He scheduled another bronchoscopy for the following day. When he went in, he determined that my throat and mouth were fine. My gastroenterologist, Dr. Kennedy, used a long skinny camera to look down my esophagus and into the stomach. She said that was all clear, actually looking the best she had ever seen it. My pulmonologist, Dr. Pryor, ordered a CT scan of my lungs and chest. The CT scan took place on *December 19, 2014, which to me was the day my life changed.*

For many months, I had a few thoughts about where the bleeding was coming from. I suspected my lungs. However, the night I had the CT scan, I had another episode of coughing up blood. After it was done, my chest hurt, and suddenly it felt like a lightning bolt shot through me. I returned to my room and told my mom, "My lungs hurt." I sat down on my bed, exhausted.

"When are we going to hear about the CT scan?" I asked. What Mom said next sent my emotions into a tailspin. Hearing the final report of the test made my muscles go limp and my heart crumble.

"You do not know this, but they already called with the results. I was not going to tell you until after the high school bowling team banquet. You know how you thought your lungs were the source?"

"Yes."

"You were right, Markus. The blood is coming from the lower part of your right lung. It is damaged and infected. The doctors think the best option is to remove that part of your lung."

At this, I lost it. We knew something was obviously wrong, but hearing those final, confirming words sent me into a huge mental and emotional breakdown. Mixed feelings started flying through me at that moment. I was thankful and relieved that we had finally figured out what was causing the bleeding. I was hopeful I would get healthy again, and I was nervous and afraid because it meant I would need yet another blasted surgery. There was no way, absolutely no way, to stop my flood of tears and shaking in that moment. I was just a ninth grader that had received some terrible news that flipped my world upside down—or so I thought.

CHAPTER 14
Markus: And High School Has Begun

Freshman year at Bloomington Jefferson High was similar to Olson in many ways. High school offered tons more elective classes that I found so amazing. It was extremely hard to choose because most of them sounded so interesting. Truly, I liked all my classes that first trimester.

In ninth grade, I had this funny social studies teacher I liked a lot. Mr. E was tall, strong, and also quite humorous. At times he would share stories from his own life, and we would all listen. High schoolers are not always such an easy crowd to captivate, but he completely had our attention.

One day I told Mr. E I was running away to go deer hunting with my Uncle Dan and would be missing class. "Don't scope yourself," was the one piece of advice he gave before I left. Of course, I did exactly that. I was kind of hoping he wouldn't see the band-aid plastered above my right eye covering stitches, but he did. When he asked what happened, I muttered, slightly embarrassed, "I got hit in the head by a shotgun scope." As Mr. E returned to the front of the room, he announced to everyone, "Class this is what happens when you don't listen to your teacher," his finger pointing at me. "Markus went deer hunting. I told him not to get scoped, and he did." Next thing I know, my classmates were clapping for me, and oh, did I ever want to duck and run. I was so embarrassed in a good way. *Now I look back and can't help but laugh.*

Yes, teachers can have a huge impact on their students. I totally looked forward to Mr. E's class. I found it humorous that when we would review assignments, Mr. E would ask, "Does anyone besides Markus know the answer?" He sounded a little weary, as if he thought no one did their homework assignment or they were not paying any attention to the task at hand. I always did my studies and made sure it was done on time, so that I knew what we were talking about. I also liked social studies. He appreciated that fact, but clearly the class I was in was kind of a quiet one, except maybe me, but not in a bad way.

Unfortunately, my freshman year was interrupted by a major surgery to remove part of my right lung. The hospital and home care filled the remainder of that school year, but I was determined to get better so I could return to high school for my sophomore year.

CHAPTER 15

Markus: Saying Good-Bye to My Lower Right Lung

The lung removal had been scheduled for the end of January. I had appointments with both Dr. Pryor, my pulmonologist, and with Dr. Anderson, my life-long surgeon. When I asked my pulmonologist about what I had and what the CT showed, he said he was appalled by what he saw. He has seen my lungs sick, but he had not seen them this bad. The solution to solve this was black and white—a surgery to remove the diseased portion of my right lung. The name of the disease that was and is rampant in me, is called *bronchiectasis*.

I know what pneumonia is because I often fell sick with that, but bronchiectasis? Bronch-ee-ecta-WHAT??? I had no idea what that was.

Bronchiectasis is a disease that affects a person's lungs and trachea by making them weak and floppy. Healthy lungs have some rigidity to support the structure of the airways. Even if a person coughs, the lungs stay open enough to clear stuff out. However, a person who has bronchiectasis has a hard time coughing junk up and out because the airway tubes want to collapse, as do the tiny air sacs, making it hard for them to stay open. This can cause other problems, mainly secretions being stuck in the lungs. Whatever cannot be cleared sits in the lungs and collects all kinds of pathogens. Those nasty guys cause havoc, and next thing you know, whatever germs that are too stubborn to leave can decide to "have a party." Excuse me, who invited them? Not me, for sure, because spending time around them makes me feel like crap. So annoying. Bronchiectasis is caused by having repetitive infections that can, and at times do damage the lungs each time that you get ill. It is a chronic lung disease right now and, unfortunately, a progressive one that will forge ahead. At what rate it will continue its path of destruction, I do not know. For me, it had advanced a fair amount over the past few months.

On January 27, 2015, at age 15-and-a-half, I was admitted to Children's Minnesota in St. Paul to say goodbye to most of my right lung forever. Dr. Anderson, my surgeon, and one of his colleagues removed my lower right lobe and what appeared to be a small, gnarled middle lobe of the right lung. Both were severely infected. "Shot" is how I would describe the condition of my right lung. The surgery itself was successful, but I did have complications. Due to the massive amount of infection in the right lung, some of it spilled out as the diseased portions were removed. The doctors did their best to suction and clean it out. I came out of surgery with two chest tubes and a ventilator.

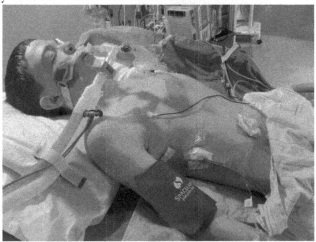

Markus, 15, after partial removal of right lung (January 2015)

January 28, 2015 (Mom's post on CaringBridge)
Recovery Day 1
Not gonna lie. This is hard, but that was to be expected. Markus will remain on the ventilator and very sedated today. Heather is sitting next to him right now playing the music on her computer from Markus's "songs I wish to be played at the hospital" list. It is very helpful to listen to the music that has brought Markus so much joy and comfort.

January 29, 2015 (Mom's post on CaringBridge)
Recovery Day 2
Markus has been "asleep" now for a little over two days. Just . . . feels . . . so . . . much . . . longer. It is good to remind myself that it is only day 2.

I had the ventilator for three days before I was ready to have it removed. Two days later a third chest tube was inserted into the empty space that had previously housed two-thirds of my right lung. The chest tubes allowed accumulated air and fluid around my lungs to safely escape my chest. Obviously, the sedation was pretty massive until the ventilator was out. I can recall "waking up" twice. One time, I could hear Pastor Jeff's voice. He prayed before I fell back asleep. Next time I came around, I thought I could see my dad's parents visiting. Otherwise, there is nothing. The knockout drug use was tapered off three days later. I had started the road to recovery, *but it was going to be a long, difficult one.*

I was on pretty good pain management, but ouch, it snuck through at times and made things unbearable. Having three chest tubes and a massive incision that ran from under my right armpit to my spine did not help! Neither did being super weak and fatigued. Mainly all I could do was lie in bed. While I was in the ICU, I was told by a pulmonologist that it would be about six weeks before I would feel comfortable again, but my pre-surgery stamina would take six months to come back. The short, white-haired lung doctor was spot-on.

With great joy, six days later, I was able to have the huge chest tube in my left side removed. What a massive relief when that first one came out. The second chest tube was removed the following day, leaving me with only one remaining in my right lung area. We tried twice to remove the final chest tube. The first time we tried, it backfired. The increased pressure squeezed my chest. The tube had to be unclamped to drain the fluid. It can be very discouraging when the progress of health-related things *do not follow our self-set timeline.* I have learned to tell myself that "such and such might happen on this day." It is totally necessary, best actually, to put the emphasis on *might.* Not easy to do in that moment when waiting is the only option.

February 8, 2015 (Mom's post on CaringBridge)
Markus asked to listen to the song "Blessings" by Laura Story a lot yesterday morning after he was told the chest tube needed to stay in. He said it helped remind him that God does not ever tell us that life will be all easy and stuff, but He does promise to see us through. It was so heartbreaking to see him cry, but he needed to before he could go on to mentally deal with the fact that the pain was not going away soon.

A couple of days later, the doctors clamped the tube again, waited twenty-four hours, and then pulled that one out. A sea of relief washed over me when that final tube came out on day 14. One by one the bonus issues that arose—fevers, nausea, anemia, and so on—were dealt with, and finally, three-plus weeks later, I was discharged to go home with IV medications.

Yes, I was home, but I was certainly not done healing. Fevers, fatigue, discomfort, and the occasional unwelcomed nausea remained. Also, I faced a marathon total of ten weeks on the IV medications. Thankfully, though, I was not coughing up blood. In fact, I had not coughed up any since the procedure, and that was a great thing for all of us. Now I could start to get back into my old routine and lifestyle. However, it was clear that I would not be returning to school to finish up my freshman year.

Having not done homework for three weeks, I had a LOT of catching up to do. For someone who truly enjoys turning in assignments early, it was overwhelming at first. I could not do much because my mental energy would tank fast. As the days went by, I slowly gained more stamina and could concentrate for longer stretches. I eventually finished my assignments, and then tackled my final semester doing online courses and packets. Thank God for homebound services.

Now summer had truly begun, and it would turn out to be a spectacular one.

CHAPTER 16
Markus: The Gift Known as Summer 2015

S ummer in Minnesota is a season of great beauty that begins the second that the snow shovel gets swapped out for a lawnmower. Hennepin County Fair was the first event on the calendar for what would be an awesome school break. Projects for 4-H had filled my free time during the long months of recovery, and now, it was time to show them at the fair. My large poster board display portrayed the growth of a litter of adorable white baby bunnies I had raised. Pictures and documentation outlined that these little balls of cottony fluff gained an average of one ounce each day. It was incredible to witness their physical growth and motor skill improvements that occurred literally every twenty-four hours. Their cuteness and personalities blossomed even faster.

Rabbit agility, breed show, and showmanship rounded out my other livestock entries. I liked to do it all. Photography was my other 4-H passion, particularly subjects like vintage cars and animals. In the end, my animal exploration project and a rabbit demonstration speech both earned trips to the Minnesota State Fair held at the end of August. It was only June, and the phenomenal summer of 2015 had begun.

My family traveled to Aunt Denise and Uncle Ed's cabin in Wisconsin. Their lake home is located on a crystal clear, quiet lake surrounded by a peaceful forest. We spent time being together, including fishing, swimming, and watching for loons and eagles on relaxing pontoon rides. Fishing is one of my all-time favorite things to do. I love trying to catch fish, especially those stubborn bass and northern pike. Splashing around in the lake is nice, but I often get frozen and blue quickly, so my actual amount of time spent in the water is limited. However, with a life jacket securely strapped on, I tried to leisurely paddle out to the water trampoline. Even though the black cover that's stretched tightly over the floating yellow tube calls out to be jumped on, I found it quite difficult. My legs have a tricky time balancing, with the water moving and all. It was best for me to sit, relaxing while the sun warmed me up at the same time. Otherwise, I am not much of a swimmer. Truth be told, I am more of a "sinker" due to my lack of body fat and weak lungs. Even so, I do enjoy hanging out at any lake.

We tried to travel as much as we could. One adventure led us to the small town of Clara City, Minnesota. One of my favorite musical performers, Mark Schultz, was holding a concert at a local church. On the way, we took the time to stop for a photo of Noah and me standing next to a statue of a giant ear of corn. We learned that Olivia, Minnesota is the "seed corn capital of the world." They are letting everyone know by displaying one huge yellow-and-green fiberglass cob of corn. Of course, we smiled and thought it was a great sightseeing opportunity.

The roads in Clara City were not bottlenecked with traffic, nor were there airplanes flying low. The brick church did not look all that big through my eyes, but it was packed. I could not hold back the thrill bubbling inside that I was at an actual concert. It is one thing to hear the music on a CD, but completely different to see with my own eyes the musician coordinate singing with playing the piano. The music that inspired and encouraged me came to life that evening.

July 18, 2015 (Mom's post on CaringBridge)
On Thursday, July 9, we were able to make a road trip to Clara City, Minnesota, to see a concert by Mark Schultz. With Mr. Schultz singing live and Markus singing next to me, I could not help but remember. Remember Markus on that ventilator, so still and quiet. The painful, difficult moments that followed when Markus asked for his music to be played. The quiet afternoons spent healing. And here was Markus, smiling and singing and praising God! It was a beautiful evening.

It felt so good, so right, to be able to personally thank Mark Schultz for sharing his gift of music.

In July, we made our annual trip to Villard to be at the lake with Mom's side of the family. My grandparents, uncles, aunts, and cousins all join together for a week of relaxing fun. We have a few traditions that happen only during that special week. The first is our family's own fishing contest. The tournament winner is determined by the heaviest or the longest fish of any species caught in Lake Villard. What is the grand prize? The coveted trophy is a boat-shaped picture frame with a photo of the winner holding the lunker of the week. Also, a weathered yellow hat sporting the name of the resort on it is yours for the remaining year. Oh, and of course, bragging rights! The following summer, it's up for grabs again. I won it once when I was eight. Even though it has been quite a while, I hold dear that esteemed honor.

With my Uncle Dan's help, I managed to catch a six-and-a-half-pound dogfish. My uncle and I were casting a black spinner lure off the end of the dock for fun. While I was reeling in, much to my shock, a brick suddenly dropped on my line. Hard as I tried,

I could not budge the crank at all, as if it was permanently cemented. My 8-year-old twig-like arms had met their match.

"Hellllppp!" I yelled in excitement.

Uncle Dan put his hands over mine to be sure I had securely hooked whatever had grabbed my bait. Without reeling the line much, we walked off the dock and onto dry land, carefully dragging that monster onto the sandy beach. The big fish got my family's attention, and some pictures were snapped of the two of us holding one crazy huge fish. (It was about as long as I was tall!) It was the only time I ever won the Villard fishing contest. Nonetheless, winning it is not the highlight of the whole competition. I truly enjoy getting the experience of going fishing and being with the family. My uncle argues that he should have had the award as well for helping me catch that big guy. He wears a smile every time he teases me about this. It's true; I could never have landed that fish on my own.

A second tradition at the lake is that we all take turns cooking dinner for the family. We have quite a crowd there, anywhere between twenty and thirty people, so lots of food is required to feed everyone. Nana and Papa usually do the first full day's dinner; then, Mom and her siblings each cook one night. The last night is, of course, leftovers. We have been doing this every year for a long time. Each evening Nana brings out her plastic tablecloths to cover four picnic tables that the adults arrange in a long line. To me, the best part is that we all sit together, chatting and laughing.

After dinner, most of us would abandon the dinner table, grab our fishing poles, bait, lifejackets, and run for the fishing boats. Dad and I would usually scamper across to the other side of Lake Villard to a popular bass and northern pike area. I loved trying to go for "the big boys" when we went out. The thing that annoyed me, even as a teenager, was that it seemed like I could not hook one of those dummies. I might have been able to snag a couple, but they either spat out the hook or pulled me into the weeds. Otherwise, I could not find that sweet spot to hook them and bring them in. Oh, well. Maybe this year, and with more practice, I can get one.

Markus, 10, wearing the coveted yellow hat with Uncle Dan

I love going to Villard for that special week with my family in July. It is the week that we Bachman kids look forward to the most. The resort has had massive changes during the decades that my family has been vacationing there. The original cabins were built in the early 1900s. They were small, but super simple and sweet. My family and I stayed in a cabin that was attached to the one my grandparents rented. We would simply walk across the old, split-wood deck to their place every morning for breakfast. We also had dinner on that old deck in front of our two cabins. Sadly, the two have been renovated into one large unit. One by one, all the remaining old-style units have been torn down and replaced with modern two-story duplexes.

Gone were the simple layouts of the cabins with old retro interior furnishing and appliances, replaced by the latest and most contemporary furnishing and appliances. There were no televisions in the old cabins, but these new ones have two. We do not need to watch television during our week there. We already have enough to do that surely does not require any screens.

Most people would probably see teenagers as ones who want the latest and greatest, disregarding old things and seeing everything as bad because it is vintage or outdated. The old cabins had an appealing character. I liked them more than these new duplexes. The one thing I do find neat about the remodeled cabins is that, now when we go, my grandparents stay with us in the two-level vacation home because there is enough room. My family takes the two upstairs bedrooms, and my grandparents take the bedroom on the main level.

Sharing the same cabin with Nana and Papa means every morning we wake to the delicious smell of bacon and coffee wafting upstairs from the kitchen. Traditionally my grandparents' cabin has been dubbed "The Nana and Papa Café." Now all we had to do was walk downstairs for it. That is the one thing I like about these new cabins; otherwise, I do not care as much for them. Thankfully, we spend most of our time outdoors.

This was the year my aunt and uncle gave my younger brother, Noah, and me a pretty sweet gift. It was a trip to Casey's Amusement Park to go mini-golfing and—even more exciting—to try go-carting. What a blast, hanging out with my relatives, competing for the fastest time. In the final lap of go-carting, before we had to pull into the pit lane, I was in the lead. I glanced to the left only to see Uncle Dan pulling up, about to overtake me. I was steering towards him a little to try and slow him down, but unknown to me, my Uncle Dave was right on my left rear tire. Next thing we know, all three of us got into a tangle, and that did it—and I lost. I did not care because it was all such crazy, kid-like fun.

Some "fast-and-furious" fun

This summer was full of car fun, everything from antique car shows to test driving new automobiles. Dad and I had decided that when I was recovered enough from surgery that we would find some crazy muscle car to test drive for kicks. The weekend that only Dad and I were at home seemed the perfect time. After poking around the listings to see what was out there, we found one that interested us. It was a black 2009 Dodge Challenger R/T with gray decals, complete with a Hemi engine. We surfed around a few more minutes to see what else was out there for performance cars, but in the end, we chose the Challenger. When Dad called the dealership asking if we could test drive the Challenger for kicks, they offered to let us have it for the entire weekend. Dad thanked the salesman, but declined and said the afternoon would be more than enough for us. Next thing we know, we are driving over to pick it up. After exchanging a little info with the sales guy, we hopped into that beast—and oh, my! First off, we have never had fancy cars in our family. This car was pretty decked out with quite a few neat bells and whistles: black-and-white leather seats, touchscreen, Bluetooth, pushbutton start, and quite a few others. But the show was "on" when Dad fired the starter in that lot.

Dad and Markus driving a Chevy Camaro SS

The whole car trembled, as the monster V8 howled to life—all of its 375 horsepower rearing up, ready for launch. Dad and I looked at each other and laughed. I was like, "What the heck are we doing here in this car?" Laughing, Dad said that he felt like a little kid driving that 4,000-pound piece of metal with all that horsepower on tap. I mean, who wouldn't feel that way? We drove that thing all over the place for the next six or so hours, driving to a sporting goods store, around a couple of local lakes, and just driving without any real destination in mind. Occasionally we would hop off and then back on the highway, so we could floor the throttle getting back on. With the gas pedal floored, we were literally pinned to the back of our seats as the revs built up in that howling, monstrous V8. As the tachometer raced towards redline, it screamed, but definitely not like a little girl. We loved our time with that car, but a couple of things drove us crazy as well.

The first annoyance was the transmission. It was fine around town, but on the highway, it was forever bouncing between gears, like a confused puppy not sure where it should go. This led to the second annoyance, which was the sound inside the car. Yeah, that V8 was sweet, but due to the transmission constantly bouncing around, the sound would change with it. It would start off with a low-pitch grumble, then a high-pitch noise, then back down to a low-pitch grumble. After hearing that for six hours, our heads hurt, and we were ready to bring this bad boy back. What a fun weekend with Dad! The next week was going to be both fun and busy, albeit for different reasons.

Minnesota State Fair 4-H experience

To 4-H-ers, the first weekend of the Minnesota State Fair means showing their state fair-qualifying animals. There were cows, horses, pigs, sheep, rabbits, and more. I earned my trip there by doing a livestock demonstration. I was thrilled to be back in the livestock buildings. I was even more elated that I was bringing my beloved rabbit, Diamond, to compete in the breed show. I had hoped to bring an endangered breed to the State Fair—and here we were.

My girl, Diamond, is the only female of our four rabbits. Her breed is known as a Silver Fox, which is technically considered a meat rabbit. They are big guys, generally weighing between nine and twelve pounds. Silver Foxes are pretty, but my Diamond is truly beautiful. She is jet black with white hairs interspersed throughout her entire body, which make her appear silvery. Her flashy coat is not the only thing about her that sparkles.

Markus and his girl, Diamond

Her personality and temperament are the sweetest. To me, she almost acts like a dog, craving and seeking attention from people. She hops right up to the door of her wooden hutch whenever we are near. Instead of trying to dart away when I open the latch, she waits patiently, like I can almost hear her saying, "Back rub, please." Both amber eyes look heavy when I gently run a couple of fingers on the bridge of her large snout. The long back stays rounded even after the attention has ended. If she likes how I am petting her, she will plop on her stomach and close her eyes, like I lulled her into a slumber. Sometimes she will shove her head and nose into my hand, demanding more love. It is hard to imagine a domestic breed of rabbit being endangered, but my Diamond is one of not many. I had brought my cinnamon rabbit, Phil, to the state competition in 2014. Somehow my rusty, fairly social Phil got the runt gene because he is about three pounds short of the cinnamon breed "standard of perfection." Even so, he is the reason I joined 4-H in the first place. And now this year, I was able to bring my rare gem. I could hardly contain my excitement.

The big event of the summer had finally arrived: the Minnesota State Fair. The day before opening is wildly busy with all the vendors making their final touches. People were preparing their food trucks or getting booths up and running. Livestock handlers were bringing their animals to be checked in, and parades of massive trucks and cars with animal trailers were everywhere. When I arrived at the barn that housed the rabbits, it was even more madness. In the rabbit barn, a long line of adults and teenagers waited to have their animals cleared for competition. One sick rabbit staying in the barn could infect the entire herd. Thankfully, the lines moved fairly fast, and I was off looking for the cage assigned specifically for my rabbit.

The enormous barn was divided into two parts. One half housed numerous bleating sheep. To the right sat two distinct groups of rabbits. Closest to the main entrance was the American Rabbit Breeders Association (ARBA) group for their open competition. The 4-H rabbits were located at the opposite end, farthest from the door. A wide-open area divided the two groups. Rabbits were everywhere, easily over 300, maybe even closer to 350 rabbits on our 4-H side. The other group probably had a similar number. Walking in, I was greeted by a pretty strong smell of animals. Then again, what is a barn with animals if it does not smell a little bit like actual livestock? Thankfully, I was not in the barn long that first day. It was already late, and I had to be back bright and early every morning for the next four days.

The whole 4-H experience holds many opportunities, and I did as many as possible. My team, Hennepin County, participated in a rabbit-judging contest where we all judged six separate groups of rabbits. We also had to answer specific judging questions on various breed standards. Information could be on any of the recognized forty-nine domestic ARBA breeds. Later that day, we all walked to the swine barn to take a livestock test. This is required, and all who show their livestock must do it. Horses, cows, rabbits, all of the animal people did it. It is a big honor to do well on that test. My 4-H club, the Hennepin Hoppers, is one of the few clubs in the state of Minnesota that does rabbit agility. We set up our ramp, soft tunnels, and jumps in the 4-H building to demonstrate rabbit agility. It is fun to see the different reactions from the crowd.

Rabbit agility is basically the same as dog agility, only modified to fit rabbits. WCCO, a local news station, wanted to interview our group. I did not talk with the news people; one of my other friends, Lizzy, was our spokesperson. We all had our rabbits there, and our little mini-agility course was set. Everyone but me ran their rabbits through it—not that my Diamond was unable to do it, but she had absolutely no interest in it. Digger, my silver rabbit back home, would have been a different story. Digger loves to run and jump and has earned himself some fancy purple county fair ribbons.

"Markus, are you going to let Diamond give it a try?" asked the WCCO newsman as I held my big girl, Diamond.

My friend Lizzy, in her spunky Lizzy fashion, said, "Yeah, her job is to sit around looking pretty." It was all quite humorous, especially the craziness that happened to one of my best friends, Bobby.

As we were all getting ready and waiting to go on live television, Bobby set his leashed rabbit down in the grass, which did not go well. Brownie broke free, bolting right in the middle of the weatherman's forecast.

"Where's the rabbit police?!" the shocked weatherman proclaimed with a laugh. Thankfully, Brownie did not get too far. However, while we were getting interviewed, that rabbit sent

Bobby on another wild goose chase, only to be caught again. If there is one thing I can say about that shiny dark brown and copper-colored rabbit, it is that he sure likes to zip around. Even today, picturing that whole hilarious scene makes me smile and giggle inside.

The biggest draw to the whole week is the breed show. The excited energy flowing through the barn was already thick by seven in the morning. I was certainly thrilled and yet consciously tried to keep my expectations in check, considering I was up against over 300 other rabbits and their owners.

Diamond's group, less common large breed senior females, was up right away. She was judged against five other females in her category, placing fifth of six. Not great, but I was aware that physically she was not the best-in-show type. Some of the others in her category had extremely good, muscular builds, bright eyes, and shiny coats. I listened to the judge's comments and then returned Diamond to her cage. I stayed a while longer with my parents. We milled around nearby because the rabbit show took over two hours to complete. After the best-in-show was announced, I had to grab Diamond for part two of the day, the showmanship competition.

In showmanship, it is not the rabbit being judged, but rather the 4-H-er. Contestants are judged on their knowledge and proper handling techniques. Questions about feeding, care, different breeds, and health are all fair game. We were also required to physically demonstrate the handling and care of rabbits. Showmanship is performed in rounds. Everyone participates in the first round, but only a handful get a callback slip to the next round. I got through the first round, but what followed surprised me. After it was finished, I received fourth place for the ninth and tenth grade group. I never felt pressured or nervous at all during the showmanship and did the best I could. It felt quite exhilarating to have the medal placed around my neck. "Thank you, girl," I whispered into Diamond's long black ear. She lay on the table, being her normal, chilled self.

A livestock demonstration, basically a live presentation, was how I had qualified to bring my rabbit to state. The title of the speech was "Rabbits in Trouble," because believe it or not, certain breeds of domestic rabbits are on the edge of extinction. The exhibition took place in the cattle barn, not a bad place, but a messy and slightly loud one. Several rows of wooden benches faced the large area for presenters. In addition to the verbal presentation, we also had live examples of each of the rabbit breeds that I spoke about, so people could see them in person. My friend, Bobby, and I worked together on both the speech and demonstration staging. It was a fantastic experience. My time at the state fair had come to an end, but I was as happy as I was exhausted by all the buzz and activity. It was so much fun to be a part of that. A fabulous end to a perfect summer!

CHAPTER 17
Markus: I Hear High School Can Be Challenging...

M oving on to tenth grade, I was *so* looking forward to heading back to classes in school. In health class, a required course, I had to give a presentation. It could be about any health topic (drugs, alcohol, illnesses, human development, etc.). I chose to do my presentation on bronchiectasis, the actual lung disease attacking my respiratory system. I truly needed to know more about the disease. I learned so much—like symptoms, what it does, how it can affect you, and how it's treated or managed. Before doing the presentation, I had no idea exactly what this illness really was or what it was doing to my body. In fact, it would prove to be the most crucial information. A short time passed before this lung disease again flared up within me. At that point, returning to the high school classroom was no longer a safe option.

Every winter my health was a challenge. I would continue to get sick with something around Christmas every winter. Next thing I know, I would be in the hospital for a week recovering from whatever latest, greatest bug is floating around. After getting discharged, I would be put on homebound learning. With homebound services, I would remain a student in the public school system, but instead of attending school, a teacher would come to my home to help me catch up on all the learning I missed. I then would either go back to school or they would help me keep pace with the class from home.

It seemed like every year I had some homebound learning time. Sometimes it was short term; other times it was for months or years at a time. While in elementary and middle school, I usually did all the work on my own, and my parents would teach me the concept. Sometimes teachers would come to help me, which worked well until I got into high school. By then I needed a homebound teacher to help me with everything. I understood why it was not safe for me to attend school, but this was disappointing. I LOVE SCHOOL. I like my high school and the experiences each class offered day after day.

Fortunately, my high school years were not a total flop, thanks to my most awesome homebound teacher, Mr. Wise. He looked like a football player, more specifically, a defensive lineman. He was quite a funny character, and occasionally I would do or say something, and he would laugh, in a good way. Other times I would mumble or groan because some homework thing was driving me insane. Sometimes he would half smirk, allowing a few deep-pitch chuckles to escape.

Mr. Wise had a favorite song to sing when proofreading papers that I wrote. It was "Comma, comma, comma, comma . . ."—sang to the tune of the 1983 song "Karma Chameleon" by Culture Club. It was his special way of pointing out my affinity for the overuse of commas and run-on sentences. The rules of the written English language were not lost on this articulate, pickup-driving, outdoor-loving high school teacher. Ah, *the joys of being held accountable!*

When I ended up requiring homebound schooling services, I would first finish up all the work I missed from my winter trimester, and, after that was over, I switched to online courses and packets for my final trimester. Once I started that, I put the pedal to the metal, determined to finish up my courses. Mr. Wise would seem to say every week, "Markus, you know you are not on any time limits. You can take your time." My thought was usually, "Yeah, yeah, yeah. I get it, but I'm going to plow on, even though I am way ahead of where I need to be." In both ninth and tenth grade, I managed to finish school for the year a week before all the students in school got out, and this felt awesome. Being ahead also allowed me not to fall so far behind when those sick days popped up. Mr. Wise understood how important that buffer was to me, and he remained a true advocate at all times.

For my junior and senior years of high school, I envisioned myself doing the post-secondary enrollment option, or PSEO. It is an option for high school juniors and seniors, and it would give me the chance to start my college education while in high school. The benefits are many. Doing PSEO should save me time and a ton of money because I wouldn't have to pay for those college credits. My current goal, heading into my junior year, is to hopefully graduate high school with both my high school diploma and an associate degree. From there, I am noodling a few different options.

For a while, I had thought about maybe being a pediatric doctor, but then I was not sure I would be able to do that from a health standpoint. In fact, I know it would not work because I flat out cannot be around sick people. A Bachelor of Science degree in accounting is something else I considered. I have always been a numbers guy, and math is something that works well for me. A couple of other options that had floated through my mind had been engineering or maybe a writing degree. One cool, cool occupation I heard about that I didn't even know was a job is being a car buyer. Their only job is to buy cars for dealerships. They look all over the place and purchase cars for dealers to sell. As a car fanatic, I wouldn't even consider it work as I already pore over car listings every day with my Uncle Ed.

However, my dream job would be to work for a car magazine like *Motor Trend* or *Car and Driver*. I would love to do what they do, testing out the latest and coolest rides (Acura NSX anybody?) and then write reviews on them. They even do comparison tests of cars. I have subscriptions to both magazines. Every time I get one, I start reading it almost immediately, and then my mind drifts off into a dreamy state. Maybe one day it will be a reality, and I will be able to work for one of those magazines. At 17, it seems that life is full of endless options.

CHAPTER 18
Markus: What? A Lung Transplant???

The string of severe health problems continued to plague me for long periods of time. We had to figure out what to do. With the declining state of my health, my doctors thought it was time to look into a lung transplant. I was like, "Whaa…??? A lung transplant?! Me? I don't know about that." While I was in the hospital in January 2016, it was discovered that the bronchiectasis had come back, and this time it was on a destructive rampage throughout my remaining upper right lung, leaving that lung in a weakened state. It was super-inflamed, and tenacious mucus seemed to be trapped all the time. Steroids became a regular addition in an attempt to keep my airway open and prevent hemoptysis, a medical term that means "to cough up blood."

I was also on a BiPAP machine about eighteen to twenty hours a day to keep my rotting right lung open so I could clear out the constant crap it was producing. However, the added air pressure from the machine did not help me get rid of the infected, trapped mucus. To be straight-up honest on how I felt, at times, I was pissed and mad. Tethered by a five-foot leash to a breathing machine was not the type of life I had envisioned for myself. This was so hard. I did not want to feel down and out and throw life out the window, but I also did not want to stuff my feelings. Why couldn't I have back the life that I was living prior to the illness?!

In my more "anger-vated" times, I felt like slamming the BiPAP machine on the floor. Throwing it off Nana and Papa's third-floor balcony also crossed my mind. I imagined it crumbling into thousands of tiny, silent pieces. The breathing machine served a vital purpose, but at times it was most annoying. Knowing that I was quite sick, my doctors, my parents, and I started to explore options.

In the spring of 2016, I was referred to the University of Minnesota for a lung transplant evaluation. Dr. Pryor, my life-long lung doctor, sent all the requested documents, tests, x-rays, and whatever was needed to the doctors at the University of Minnesota. Then it was a waiting game to hear if they would consider me. The waiting time allowed me to research all that is involved with a lung transplant. One sentence read, "Lung transplant patients need to stay within thirty minutes of the hospital that did the transplant for at least three months after the initial discharge." Reading that, I was earnestly hoping the University of Minnesota would accept me, as our home was only about thirty minutes from the hospital. At the same time we were waiting to hear from the U of M, we also were waiting to hear from Texas Children's Hospital in Houston, Texas. The thought of relocating 1,200 miles from home for a minimum of four months *did not* appeal to me. Knowing that the door had not been closed on either location yet, I was hoping Minnesota would be an option.

We finally received a call that the U of M needed yet more information. We made our way over to this local, and yet foreign, hospital system. I stepped into a glass booth to do a breathing test to evaluate my current lung function. The second test I found rather interesting and quite revealing. This time, a radiologist injected radioactive dye through an IV in my arm. The physician watched the picture of my lungs unfold. The results concluded that my left lung did 88 percent of the work while my remaining upper right lung lobe did only 12 percent. In a normal person, lung function is usually around 50/50. This information was an eye-opener for me, as I knew my right lung's health was going downhill, but I did not realize the right lung was *that* dysfunctional. After what felt like a long day of tests, I returned home until our scheduled appointment.

It was strange to be in a different hospital. Up to that point, I had *always* been at Children's Minnesota. During our appointment, the University of Minnesota surgeon shared that I was not a candidate for a lung transplant. "It is a high-risk procedure, and you are a high-risk candidate." His group proposed another idea, using stents to keep my right lung open. We thought about their suggestion, but we did not have peace that this bridge would help my situation. Later, both my pediatric surgeon and pulmonologist didn't seem to agree with that idea either. Both feared that it could complicate things rather than help. Ultimately, the U of M door closed, which left Texas Children's Hospital in Houston as my other hopeful option.

April 24, 2016 (Markus's post on CaringBridge)

I'm kind of bummed out, but as long as we aren't at a dead end and we have other options, I'm willing to explore other ones. Anything to try to improve my lungs and breathing abilities.

CHAPTER 19
Markus: Lone Star State, Here We Come

A ll along, I had envisioned remaining close to home and all the people I have loved my whole life. This is probably the reason I will never forget the instant I heard the words: "We are going to Texas." It was not a whirlwind decision. It was what we had to do next, what my family was willing to do for me. So many thoughts rushed through my brain: "What will happen now? We will be so far from family and home. I just turned 17! Will we have to move? Is this really happening to me?" Of course, I was thankful and hopeful, however, the shock waves inside swirled almost out of control at times. I would say that my emotions were all tangled up in a huge ball. I could not unwind it even half an inch in order to begin describing everything I was feeling: panic, hope, the emptiness in my chest brought on by the thought of leaving all I had ever known, and yet a twinge of excitement to actually travel. We were scheduled to leave in only three weeks. Indeed, it came up quickly, and next thing we knew, Mom, Dad, Heather, 21, Noah, 10, and I were all piling into our over-stuffed minivan for the 1,200-mile drive south.

Thankfully, we broke up the drive into three days. My groin was bruised down to my knee from a cardiac catheter procedure I had undergone only one week prior to our trip. Coils were placed in a leaky collateral blood vessel that had branched off to my bad lung. Blood flow was blocked in an attempt to temporarily stop the increased bleeding. "Ouch" does not even begin to describe the stiffness I endured every ninety minutes when Dad stopped the van so I could get out and walk. Getting up and out of the van was a slow, painful chore. The first day, we drove to near Des Moines, Iowa, and stayed with some friends. Day two we made it to Oklahoma City, Oklahoma. The large state of Texas greeted us that third day. On the freeway, I could not help but notice all the pickup trucks and palm trees. It looked so different than my midwestern Minnesota dwellings. This northern boy was not used to the sweltering, unforgiving heat that rushed in every time the car door opened. I like warm, but that was way too close to boiling for me. Once we reached the hotel, we hurriedly unpacked the van and settled into what was a quite decked-out hotel room.

Mom, Dad, and I were out the door and at Texas Children's Hospital by 8:00 in the morning for the first of several tests. While we were in the waiting room to get my blood drawn, my first stop, we met another boy and his mom. To our surprise, we learned that the 16-year-old had had a lung transplant the previous month. I did not get to talk with either of them, but while I was getting my lab work done, Mom chatted with them in the waiting room.

The lab draw took less than fifteen minutes, if even. However, when I left, I felt like I was going to pass out because they drew nine vials and a syringe of blood from me in one sitting. It made my brain a little woozy, but I managed to focus on my next task, the lung function test. The pulmonary lung function test (PFT), gives a snapshot of how well the lungs are working.

The first doctor we met with was a pulmonologist, a lung doctor. We discussed my history; in fact, we talked about my history with practically everyone we met. The physician discussed the transplant option and where things were at now. It was all so much information, some of the words kind of washed over me, leaving a droplet or two here and there. A lot of what she said was too much for me to absorb and take in. After that, there was a whole lot more testing to do. We finally wrapped up day one at 5:00 in the afternoon. I was beat. Thankfully, day two would turn out to be much easier.

Only two things were on my plate for the evaluation process the next day: another lab draw and a meeting with a psychologist. A nice, easy schedule left us with a wide-open afternoon. What was the one thing all five of us wanted to do? Go to Galveston, Texas, to check out the Gulf of Mexico, of course. What a gorgeous sight it was! The streets were lined with palm trees, something I am not used to seeing because we do not have them in Minnesota. The large, flat, swaying leaves and trunks looked pretty neat to me. However, they also served as a distinct visual reminder of this unfamiliar tropical climate. This was certainly not my "land of 10,000 lakes."

Living in Minnesota, our summers are usually in the high 70s to 80s, with an occasional 90-degree day. Humidity is not always high, which is quite nice. In Texas, it was already in the 80s and humid by 8:00 in the morning. By midafternoon, it was on its way to mid-90s. It was a very humid 90 degrees, and it felt like it was over 100 practically every day. I usually stayed inside most of the time. Texas's weather and temperatures made me feel like I was in a furnace or oven set on high when I was outside, and I sure did not enjoy it. In fact, I do not think any of us much cared for the heat. Staying indoors, though, was not our plan at the gulf.

When we arrived at the beach, we were greeted by sights of the gulf: people and tons of birds swooping everywhere. The five of us clambered onto the beach. I was expecting the normal rough grittiness of the lake beaches back home. What a surprise! The sand was smooth and powdery, almost silky, under my startled toes. In fact, it was downright amazing. The water was also another pleasant surprise.

Swimming is a challenge for me. It is too much for my lungs, and ultimately, I flat-out sink. When I do swim, it is like the water kicks me out because it is way too cold for me. I will almost always turn blue, but that did not happen in the gulf water. Sure, I did not have to deal with cold water, but I had to try and keep my balance against some powerful and slightly turbulent waves that nearly knocked me off my feet. I did not get slammed over, but Mom and Heather did. We were all having a good old time, laughing together as a family, which is a challenge for us at times due to my health struggles and the frequent illnesses that don't seem to want to leave me alone. Drying off under the Texas sun was such a wonderful, new sensation. I did not shiver once. Warming on my towel, I decided to take the opportunity to capture some images in this unique setting. Most of my photos were of the numerous birds all over the beach, although I did take a couple of photos of my family. There was also one of a crab. Never saw one of those guys before. After a quick, very memorable few hours at the gulf, we had to say goodbye to Galveston.

Wednesday was another fairly busy day, but it was not terrible, just more appointments with various people. We met with an infectious disease doctor, pharmacist, the surgeons, and a few others. After they were all completed, we had enough spare time and energy to explore the mall next door to the hotel.

The Galleria, as it is called, was huge. Its immense size took up two entire city blocks. All five of us went there to do some souvenir shopping as well as check it out. To me, a lot of the stores in that mall seemed to be high-end, expensive stores with fancy, opulent merchandise. In fact, one of those fancy-looking stores was a Tesla shop. Since I am a car nut, of course, I had to get a picture with those sleek-looking electric cars. However, our goal was to get some things to remind us of our time in Texas. The tourist store was lined with various clocks shaped like the state of Texas, Texas t-shirts, picture frames, mugs, keychains, postcards, and other small items. I had never been to a souvenir shop before, so I chalked this one up to a unique type of experience. Glad we did it.

Day four, Thursday, was another busy one. I had one more test and a bunch of meetings. I honestly cannot recall much from every appointment, as so much information was being thrown at me. Not that I did not listen to them, but I really could not absorb everything they said. The process is a long one, and there is a lot of information to be gathered and learned. I have heard the saying, "Like trying to get a drink from a fire hose." The stuff kept coming at me so fast, I was drenched with information and ready to push it to the back of my mind for another day. As much as I looked forward to getting home, I will always be immensely grateful for the recommendations offered by my new southern doctors.

Texas Children's Hospital is extremely big, so big, in fact, it has two parts. One is seventeen floors tall, and the other is twenty-one floors. Now, one would think that the traffic inside that large a building would not be too bad, right? Well, it was awful. There were six elevators in that hospital, and at times it took ten to fifteen minutes to get on one that had enough room for more people. Also, it was so packed that it seemed like people were swarming every single level of that hospital. Dad went so far as to call it "rush hour."

However, I saw a whole lot of other kids like me who had their own health problems—lots of kids with trachs, feeding pumps, oxygen support, as well as kids in wheelchairs, kids on ventilators, and a whole lot more. Seeing them reminded me that I certainly am not the only kid with a medical problem. No, here was a whole hospital and community of kids and teenagers with complex health issues, and they were also looking for help, just like me. Thankfully, all the people we crossed paths with were quite friendly, thorough, and even comical at times.

On day two of the evaluation, a broad-chested, animated lab guy bellowed in a southern accent, "Markus! Greatest name in the world!" I broke out laughing at his booming enthusiasm that was loud even to my mostly deaf ears. Turned out the lab tech's name was also Marcus, albeit with a "c," and not a "k." Go figure! That would explain his abundance of enthusiasm, knowing we both belong to the same-name club. Marcus #1 got Markus #2 with the first stick. He chatted about being raised in "backwoods Louisiana." Growing up swimming with 'gators, swampin' for crawdads, froggin', and looking for turtles sounded both like a dangerous, yet absolutely amazing, adventure. His grandma had raised a baby turtle for a year to fatten it up, and then she made turtle soup. I hardly noticed the blood leaving my arm listening to him chatter.

Another laugh-out-loud episode happened during a bone-density scan. I went into the empty cube of a room. It contained a computer, two chairs, a bed for me to lie on, and the x-ray machine. The equipment moved up and down my body as well as side to side, creating a complete, detailed picture. I was dressed for the occasion in one of those ugly, uncomfortable, often-breezy hospital gowns. At least I got to wear my own shorts; however, I totally forgot to check my pockets before we started. The radiologist was watching the picture unfold, and she was alarmed when she saw a little round lump on my left side. The tech pointed it out to my dad. Dad smiled as he asked me, "Do you have something in your left pocket?"

"Oh, crap! Yes, I do." That lump in the picture was a bouncy ball I had gotten earlier that day for my younger brother. I totally forgot that I had put it in there until it came up on the x-ray. The radiologist ended up laughing when she saw it was simply a toy. I was slightly embarrassed at myself, though, for overlooking that detail. Thankfully, it was far enough away from my body that we did not have to take another picture, which was a relief for me. Houston definitely held some humorous moments.

June 23, 2016 (Markus's post on CaringBridge)
All of the medical stuff (below) is typed in Mom's words and not mine. Sorry! Too much for me to digest, and Mom is better at recapping all this medical stuff from the evaluation.

Medical stuff/Evaluation . . . Learned so much this week. Some of the best news came after an ultrasound this morning on Markus's groin/right thigh area. It has been painful since the cardiac cath and it developed a HUGE, dark, deep purple bruise. Ask me if you want to see the picture, otherwise, I will spare you. Good news is it is just that, a bruise, also known as a hematoma. We spent the last couple weeks hoping it was not an aneurism caused by the cath procedure. Such a relief.

Markus needs to revisit a lot of his immunizations, especially the new pneumonia vaccines that are offered. His bones are in a weakened state, so we need to keep trying to wean off the prednisone and do more weight-bearing exercises. Doctors here thought his right lung "looks bizarre" on an x-ray. They commented that it looked like there was an implant in the space where the lung used to be. Best they could tell, the area below his lung is filled with air and they said it was good that we drove (instead of flying).

The surgeon said that a lung transplant, for Markus, "has a fair amount of uncertainty and high risk. Looks like things could be dealt with." He shared a laundry list of concerns regarding surgery for Markus and his anatomy. We will hear the final recommendations from the team within ten days. I can say this much, Markus will not be getting a transplant today or tomorrow. It is a huge thing, has possible great outcomes, but also possible complications and huge risks. Discussed quality of life and life-limiting conditions and whew! Nobody wants to talk about those things or dwell on them. We all are grateful to start heading home tomorrow.

During the meeting with the surgeon, an option was proposed that I knew was a definitive "no way, never going to happen." The possible solution involved getting a trach again, but this time, the top of my airway would be permanently stitched shut. The tall physician explained that this would completely eliminate any connection between the airway and stomach to prevent reflux from ever soiling new lungs. Choosing this path would end my ability to speak audibly. And getting a trach again? This time forever? All I could do was slowly shake my head side to side.

In the end, our trip to Houston turned out to be most helpful. The southern doctors were able to give my Minnesota physicians some beneficial suggestions. When we received the final report, we learned that I was not a candidate for a lung transplant at Texas Children's Hospital. Severe gastric reflux was cited as one factor. Transplanted lungs do not respond well to any potential spillage from stomach acid. A second major concern was the possibility that transplanted lungs would not attach and heal properly with my unique anatomy. For these reasons, a new set of lungs was not an option. This was undeniably both good and bad news. The best, actually amazing, news was hearing the surgeon say, "The left lung actually looks pretty good. Why would we want to remove it?" Transplant is a treatment option, but only when there is no other option. What was my other option?

CHAPTER 20
Markus: So What Now?

Since a lung transplant was no longer possible, thoughts about getting one stopped. Being the one who was struggling with a failing lung, I was frustrated. What else could I possibly do to rid my body of something that doesn't really belong? When I felt like our toolbox was getting smaller, my doctor came up with a solution: remove the remainder of my right lung.

My doctors had pondered this before, but wanted to be sure it would not limit future possibilities of transplant options. In May 2017, around my eighteenth birthday, I experienced yet another episode of double-lung pneumonia. I was an utter mess with that illness. So many different bugs were causing this illness that it was very scary, especially as the number of effective drugs began to shrink. The infectious disease doctors following my case said the right lung was too far gone and had to come out. At that point, I agreed that this had to get done. I was fed up with getting seriously sick so often.

Each ensuing medical appointment mainly focused on some aspect of the lung surgery. During appointments with my lung doctor, we'd talk about what I would want and not want. I didn't want to wait much longer. I was adamant about the fact that I did not want a tracheostomy. I had had one for eight-and-a-half years and had been free of it for almost ten years. Dr. Pryor, my lung doctor, said he clearly got it and told me, "I don't think we'd be doing this if we didn't think your left lung could support you without help." His comment made sense to me, thinking back to the test that showed my left lung carried the bulk of the work. Another non-negotiable point we agreed on was it would all take place at Children's Minnesota Hospital in Minneapolis.

The whole medical game changed the day I turned 18—the magical age when I am legally responsible for my own healthcare decisions. Thing is, I already had had a total say in everything for years. Since I was a minor, I had never signed the oh-so-many forms. Two weeks before my official adult birthday, my uncle, parents, and I had lengthy discussions about healthcare directives and power of attorney, not fun stuff to think about, but extremely important. Being laid up with pneumonia, legal documents were the last thing on my mind. They were in the works per previous discussions, but there is always time, right? I mean, what could go wrong?

June 1, 2017 (Markus's post on CaringBridge)
14 days now here at Minneapolis Children's. Ugh!

Good/fun stuff. This section isn't going to be as long because I've been here at the hospital for quite a while, but I have done some nice things. To kill time, I've mainly been doing stuff on my iPad, reading some, visiting with people, talking with people over the phone, and watching TV. Been watching all types of stuff: Animal Planet, Food Network, Mecum Auto Auctions, to name a few, and also playing Bingo, which the hospital offers three days a week.

However, two big things have been fun. On Saturday, the doctors allowed me to attend a wedding that I really wanted to go to so much. The big reasons were because the bride is my sister's best friend from high school, and also, Heather was in the wedding as a bridesmaid. Because of these, I desperately wanted to go, and I was given permission.

The second one is leaving me psyched to the point I JUST WANT TO GET HOOOMMMEEE!!! This surprise came Tuesday (and yesterday, Wednesday), and because of it, I'm DYING to get outta here!! Behind my back (no lie; they didn't tell me anything about this until they were actually doing it!), my parents signed a two-year lease on a brand-new Ram 1500. Dad brought it up here to the hospital last night so I could see it. Now that I've seen it, I'm itching to get out of here and behind the wheel of that truck. At least I have something to look forward to upon getting out of here. And no, it's not MY truck. It's going to be driven by me and my parents as a family vehicle.

Unfortunately, there's quite a bit of not-so-good news here. First off, the nasty fevers haven't released their grip. I was fever free from Sunday until yesterday morning, and then they came back with a vengeance. Last Friday I had a 103.1 temp that broke Sunday but returned yesterday. Last night I had a 102.6 temp. I felt horrible. I was shaking so violently and uncontrollably that it gave me an eerie flashback to fourteen days ago when I woke up with uncontrollable shaking and the fever that landed me here. The coughing hasn't improved a whole lot. After all of the tests were run, it was determined I have pneumonia. At first, only my right lung was infected. Unfortunately, now both are. Also, I have been at a stalemate and haven't made much progress, so I am having my lungs washed out (suck the junk out of the lungs) tomorrow at 1:30. Not happy about that, but hopefully it'll get me somewhere. Also, we've run into problems finding medicines that will treat what's going on, as several have come back as ineffective at this point. A final thing is that my port has been seriously acting up. At least three times in the last week or so, this lifeline seems like it's going to quit on me. Thankfully, with an agent injected to clear the line, we've kept it open enough that it remains functional.

Please pray the procedure goes smoothly. Last time I had this done, I ended up on a ventilator and was knocked out for about twenty-four to thirty-six hours. Please pray they find answers and the right ones (like an "aha" moment, perhaps) to deal with this. Pray for improvements in my health, as I feel like I'm not making any progress and would love to make progress. For the fevers to break and stay away! Pray for my coughing to subside. Please pray my left lung can recover from this quickly, and there is no damage to it as there is more serious talk of removing the rest of my right lung. Please pray that my IV will stay open and functional, and not be a pain in my rear end.

(End of post)

▶ ▶ ▶ ▶ ▶

Trouble was, the ventilator could not be immediately removed after the lung wash. Being knocked out, well, I could not give them my permission for anything. And with the healthcare directive papers not yet signed by me, neither could the two people I trust the most—my parents. What a messy deal! Doctors had to contact their hospital lawyers for how to proceed. Yikes! Fortunately, things worked out and, as soon as I was lucid and physically able, I signed those legal documents. I now had vital protections in place, and other people were clear on my healthcare choices. Eventually, I was discharged and moved forward with other medical appointments.

Surgeons discussed specifics, risks, and what to expect. Dr. Anderson, my pediatric surgeon, always tells me he needs a "Plan A, B, C, so on and so forth" because I am a unique case (to somewhat quote him). According to Dr. Anderson, I don't exactly follow the norm for surgical patients. Henceforth, he makes multiple back-up plans. Now that I am an adult, he also brought an adult thoracic surgeon on board. With my first doctor for "grown-ups" now on the scene, it all seemed set. November it would be "a go," and all six of my necessary specialists would be there.

Funny thing is, plans can change, and sometimes that is good, really good. A week before my scheduled date, Dr. Anderson called us. He and my other doctor were talking about my situation at lunch when some cardiac thoracic surgeons, whom I had never met, joined them. When the other surgeons suggested a different approach, all my doctors agreed. Was that a random encounter over sandwiches? I do not think so. Now seven specialists would be there—and it was a go.

CHAPTER 21
Mom: Lung Removal, Round 2

We knew something drastic had to be done to stop what was happening in Markus's airway. A second lung-removal surgery was the only logical option remaining. Our son had been through so much in his years, and now again he was facing a second lung-removal operation. If he survived, there would be no more lung-removal options. This was it. Markus could have said no, but he was not ready to quit, and neither were we.

On my birthday, Dr. Anderson called with the news of a different surgical approach. The plan had completely changed. All the new groundwork had been carefully placed, and every detail, including Dr. Anderson meeting with the entire surgical crew, was in motion. Everything that could be planned, discussed, and prepared was in order. Looking back, some large, life-altering moments had occurred on my birthday, November 3. Incredibly enough, after five months and eight days in the NICU, Markus came home from the hospital as an infant. I woke up the following morning with my son at home for the first time . . . *on my birthday.*

At eight-and-a-half, Markus had his trach tube removed at the hospital and came home the next day . . . *on my birthday.* The hole in his throat was still there, but now we could see the delicate skin covering his entire neck while he breathed through his nose.

Breath after breath, I could feel small amounts of air being exhaled from his nostrils for the first time.

November 4, 2016 (Mom's old post on CaringBridge)
Sorry Markus, but at times a mom has to pipe in. Just ask Heather, hard as I try, I do catch myself saying "Mom stuff" to her at 22. Usually, we girls smile, giggle, and even belly laugh. Here goes . . .

It is 4:30 a.m. right now on Friday, November 4. Markus is finally asleep again in the bed across the room from me. Things had been improving for him, which basically means that he was coughing up less and less blood. Wednesday evening took a disheartening turn for him. There was a large increase in the brighter blood as his treatments were ending. It was a frustrating moment for him and understandably so. We prayed. We cried. I later found my husband, Mike, upstairs on the couch, head in his hands. It was crushing.

Yesterday morning, Thursday, November 3, I did not know what to expect. I was greeted by a bright-eyed, smiling Markus. He was ready for the day and more than ready to start schoolwork. There was not even a hint of the sadness or frustration of the prior evening. Next was Mike, hugging me, reminding me to stay in the moment, to LIVE this day. Seeing both guys this morning with such determination, focus, and joy was the best gift I could have asked for. You see, yesterday, November 3, was my birthday.

(End of post)

▸ ▸ ▸ ▸ ▸

Such precious gifts could only come from one source. The change in surgical strategy was something I would not have even known to ask for, but it was the exact present we needed for our Markus. It was an invisible yet deeply felt poke in the ribs—a timely "Hey, I see you" that triggers a deep, deep breath and reminds me of the importance of being still.

Not that the week before surgery was uneventful. Markus coughed out a lot of blood, so much that he was admitted to the hospital. Glimpses of frustration that we rarely see came from inside my boy.

"I simply wanted to spend these last nights at home," Markus repeated. He did get two nights at home, which for him, was truly enough.

"I am ready," he said calmly as he was admitted to the cardiovascular intensive care unit one night earlier than planned. Everything about Markus confirmed that *he was just that—ready.* Late that night I listened to him talking to the night nurse, sharing his thoughts, his story. He knew how risky this would be. He remembered the pain and recovery struggles from the previous lung removal. Yet here he was, talking, not crying, not screaming or panicking. I wanted to cry as I begged God to spare him, to protect my son. Time for crying and lamenting would come, but for now, I had to, I needed to be present with him and walk through each moment.

November 9, 2017 (Markus's post on CaringBridge)

Well, I was able to check off what I wanted to do the last couple of days at home. I was able to attend the bowling banquet, get some last-minute homework done, and at least be home with the family for two nights.

Now I'm back at Children's Minnesota a day early. I was coughing up bright red blood, so back to the hospital I went. Oh well. They did the x-ray this morning, and good news about that showed that the left side is clear and good—which means surgery is on for tomorrow at 7:30 a.m. My hemoglobin is good, and I feel normal, except for the coughing up of blood.

Gonna spend my last night before surgery playing games with my family. I am leaving you with a couple songs that have been going through my mind and heart leading up to surgery. They have been "He is With You" by Mandisa and "Love Never Fails" by Brandon Heath. If you have never heard of these two songs, I'd encourage you to listen to them.

With this post, I'll be "signing off" for a while. Posts will be done later by Mom, Dad, or Heather.

– Markus

(End of post)

▶ ▶ ▶ ▶ ▶

Early morning came, and so did each physician. They all told him he was strong, brave, and an inspiration. Markus genuinely hugged and thanked them.

"You will get through this, and then we have some fish to catch," Dr. Anderson told Markus as his voice cracked. He had previously shared with us that he also enjoys being on the lake and getting a line wet.

"Absolutely," Markus replied with a grin, obviously a fan of the idea.

Once again, my husband and I brought our Markus back to the operating room—our most dreaded thing to do. Once he was asleep, then we could fall apart, pray, and ask God to please protect and spare our amazing guy. Then we waited for the occasional updates. Once I took our youngest, 11-year-old Noah, to buy food at the cafeteria. The Dude was doing a live filming of his daily show. He asked Noah some questions and found out that he was Markus's brother.

"Yo! *My buddy Markus?*" asked the Dude. Noah nodded. "Hey, this is a shout out to my friend Markus who is in surg. Get well Markus. Be seeing you soon." Later he shared that Markus could go back and view the show when he felt better. The Dude is good medicine for both my boys and even to us parents. He is gifted at helping bring smiles in some trying times.

One by one, we watched other families leave the surgical waiting area until only our family remained. My siblings took Noah for another walk to allow some much-needed time to temporarily crumble emotionally. Hours later we got the call that surgery was over, and they were closing him up. Step one, surviving the surgery, was over.

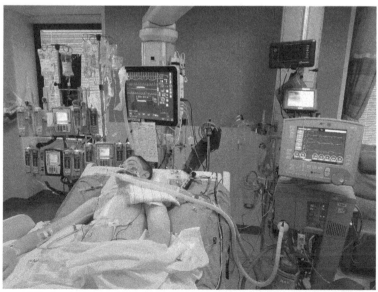

Markus, 18, after complete removal of the right lung
(November 2017)

CHAPTER 22
Mom: Recovery Round 2

Recovery has calm, peaceful moments that allow a parent to block out all the machines, stitches, and life-threatening trauma that has occurred to their child's body. It is waiting, trusting that with every second that passes, cells are repairing and healing. It is hoping that life will improve for this silent, motionless individual who is so loved and treasured. It is in these seconds I realize how little I can do to help Markus's situation. Then sometimes, minutes later, the action turns into hand-to-hand combat with an unknown, invisible enemy.

Markus had been quiet. The ventilator was in place, but nothing had been suctioned from the tube going down to his lung. This was not unusual for him. The medications keep him from moving, including coughing. Even on a regular day, Markus needed to intentionally use his muscles to mobilize lung secretions and spit them out. Vents are tricky for him.

He was being weaned off the paralyzing muscle relaxer. Slowly, Markus was being brought to a place between total sedation and wakefulness. I woke early in the morning because of commotion in the hospital room. "Mike, please check what is going on. I need my head to get steady," I asked my half-asleep husband lying next to me on the small fold-open hospital couch.

Mike went to his bedside. "Deb, come here. Markus is trying to sign something, but I cannot figure out what he is trying to say."

I ran to him. Markus's wide-open, drugged eyes were frantic with panic. He was moving his hand, three fingers over the thumb, circle, three fingers over the thumb, over and over signing: *M-O-M*. Something was very wrong. I grabbed his hand and immediately he coughed, his entire face now a deep purple. Oxygen saturations dropped to 60 and then secretions started flowing out his mouth. "He needs suctioning!" I hollered as I placed the oral suction inside his cheek, removing the sudden copious eruptions of fluid from his mouth. The nurse dragged out large amounts of thick secretions from the tube in his airway. Oxygen was increased to the ventilator. Suction airway, suction mouth, airway, mouth, repeat! So much thick stuff was pouring out. How could he breathe at all? Dark green bile flowed out the nose tube that went to his stomach. A bump in sedation calmed Markus enough to slow the tsunami of secretions and allow the vent to breathe for him. The room was once again an atmosphere of relative quiet. It was a moment that solidified my son's disdain for tubes in his throat—and increased my desire for him to get off the vent as soon as possible.

My "Mom kisses" could not heal Markus's wounds or calm this storm. My registered nurse skills could not silence the panic threatening to erupt in my brain. Even heavily sedated, he looked to me, to us, to help him. Only, I am so helpless to truly change anything.

"He needs to get off the vent. He cannot clear anything on that thing," I whispered to my exhausted husband. Even though Mike and I knew Markus had to get off the vent, it is also a terrifying thing to do. Markus is difficult to intubate, and if he did not respond well. . . I could not think about that. No matter what, it was time to execute the removal plan. And it worked, never exactly as planned, but with adaptations made as necessary. Bottom line: It worked.

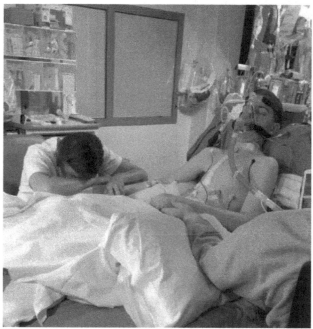

Markus, 18, lung surgery 2, off the ventilator and on BiPAP
machine while Mom and Dad hold his hands.

As with the first lung surgery, each tube was gradually
withdrawn from his long, thin body. Markus slowly regained the
strength to sit, then stand, and ultimately walk again. Two weeks
after surgery, Markus was able to walk the hospital hallways with
his dad.

November 24, 2017 (Dad's post on CaringBridge)

There's not much to share today in terms of changes in Markus,
either positive or negative. It was a good day, a quiet day. But
during one of his walks today, there was a "God moment" so
stunning that I have to share it.

For the vast majority of our lives, we don't pay much attention
to or recognize that God is there and at work. At other times, well

. . . have you ever experienced a nearby lightning strike where the flash, the boom, the electricity and shock are instantaneous and intense? That was today's encounter. We were on our way back from a walk. A vibrant, "salt-and-pepper" bearded man visiting another family spoke up as we approached. "You wanna compare scars?" Random, this question totally caught us off guard, and we didn't know how to respond. "I saw the scar. Wanna compare?" I didn't know exactly what to say as he started to tug at his shirt a little. But then I finally got words out, saying that Markus had his lung removed.

The man said, "I have only one lung, too!" BOOOOMM!

He went on to describe how, at about 18, his chronically infected right lung was removed. CRRRACK!! He then shared some of his experiences and insights since that time. We were spellbound. He spoke of things that only he and Markus could share and understand. Describing the transition to life with one lung—his limitations, freedoms, fears, illness with one lung (picture me sitting on your chest). He listened intently to Markus's questions and answered them as though he and Markus were one. But what he kept repeating was encouragement that, in our eyes, came straight from God. "Keep going! Never give up! The biggest challenges you'll face are right here (pointing to his head), but YOU CAN OVERCOME IT! Keep going!"

We ended up talking for a good ten minutes before parting ways. Markus and I hardly said a word for several minutes as we walked. But all that while, I was thanking God for putting that man, Pastor J from Le Sueur, right there, right then, to encourage Markus, to encourage us—and not as a whisper or something that might not be noticed—but as a burst, a shock that is unmistakably Him.

~Mike

(End of post)

▶ ▶ ▶ ▶ ▶

Mike stayed with Markus the entire twenty-three days until he was discharged because I, too, was sick, and could not visit the hospital. Thankfully, Mike's employer allowed him to work using his computer and cell phone when quieter moments allowed him the necessary focus. He shared each day's news as I coughed at home. My husband, since the beginning of Markus's life, showed me sides of him that I never knew existed. His steadfast commitment to each of us, his care for others he did not even know, and his quickness to forego his own comfort have been evident over and over. Markus certainly hit the jackpot when it comes to his dad.

CHAPTER 23
Mom: Doubt? Oh, Me of Little Faith!

Heather was given muscle, coordination, and a six-foot-three frame to boot. Markus adores his big sister and has always been her biggest fan. Volleyball, basketball, golf, you name it, she tried it, and it all came naturally to her. Markus was more excited than Heather when college coaches called and sent her stacks of letters.

"I want to get an athletic scholarship!" Markus would share.

His sport of choice in the early years was by far basketball. We had a hoop in the driveway. Neighbor kids would spend hours shooting baskets, playing "Horse," "Lightning," anything basketball. In Lightning, Markus was more often than not the first person out, but that did not matter to him. He was back in line the moment a new game began.

Back when he had a trach, Markus had played two years of baseball, which he was pretty good at. The problem was the brown dust clouds that quickly became airborne when little athletes kicked at the dirt. A most natural thing to do at any age, but for Markus playing baseball was not safe. The hole in his throat bypassed the natural filtering system of the nose. Baseball was out. Our hometown of Bloomington has a city golf program for youth. Markus so enjoys swinging the clubs, so we let him give it a try.

Turns out, golfing with his dad, Grandpa Gene, nurse Kevin, and other family was a lot more fun. I agree.

Somehow Markus convinced us to sign him up for youth basketball during fifth grade. There might have been a little begging involved. Unfortunately, his health was not a fan of the sport. It was the fastest I've ever seen him move. As in everything, he gave 120 percent. Once he put up a shot that rolled on the rim. It did not go in, but it was close. It was an almost, so, so close, and that put quite a smile on his face.

During a different game, Markus was given the opportunity to play point guard for one quarter. As soon as he dribbled the basketball over the half-court line, the other guard immediately stole that orange and black ball and took off running. Time after time Markus brought the ball up the court and the opponents quickly snatched it away. A mom sitting next to me became quite annoyed at the other coach for not telling his players to back down. At this point, I think the adults who recognized Markus's medical situation were feeling bad for him. Interestingly enough, I did not. I was witnessing resilience and a spirit in my son that would not give up. Each time he approached that line smiling, determination intact, switching things up and even trying to dribble the ball with his weak right hand. "You got this Markus. That's it," cheered his coach over and over. As a mom, it was a completely amazing sight, one I am not entirely sure I was able to explain well to the other parents. He was definitely not a star player, but he was our star, radiating his Markus ways far beyond any gymnasium floor. I am grateful he had the opportunity, but the day after a game, he was often too sick for school. Basketball was not his calling.

The ideal match for my athletic wannabe turned out to be bowling. The high school bowling team, the schedule, the skill set was a perfect fit for this guy. He developed a trained, effective style to his delivery. It was an absolute winner. The team camaraderie and genuine friendships were surprise bonuses. The bowling community treated Markus as an equal. These people did not fear or avoid him, but instead, they embraced him. Younger brother Noah even got to practice with Markus's high school team during his senior season. In my mind, this could be about the best thing ever, but Markus had grander ideas. "I want to get an athletic scholarship for bowling."

Deep breath. How do I respond? He would occasionally throw games over 200, but he was probably not going to make the All-Conference Team. None of that mattered to him, or to us. Why not dream big? I mean, did I ever imagine myself spending four hours on Saturday afternoons cheering for bowling? No, but we did. And it turned out to be fun. No referees for parents to criticize. We did not witness any life-altering injuries. The competing teams high-fived and encouraged each other during matches, even when the score was tied in the tenth frame. "Anything is possible," I said.

Markus bowling for his high school

Born Again Jocks is a sports organization in our hometown of Bloomington for athletes 55 and older. They participate in all types of sports. To say this group of health-minded individuals is inspirational is an understatement. The Born Again Jocks volley-ball team used to scrimmage Heather's high school varsity team. It is no surprise that these 70- and 80-year-old athletes beat the high schoolers. What a great experience for all those high school juniors and seniors to see that people can compete *at any age.*

Born Again Jocks is an active community that offers a scholarship to high school seniors based on athletic participation, community involvement, and academics. I shook my head in amazement the day Markus received the letter congratulating him as one of the scholarship recipients. "Looks like you did get that athletic scholarship, Markus!" I congratulated this remarkable young man. What a fabulous honor!

The Optimist Club is another group in Bloomington that has a scholarship program. They sponsor an oratorical and written essay contest based on a given topic for students ages twelve to seventeen as well as a speech competition for youth with hearing issues. The local club sponsored Markus to attend the district competition in South Dakota. The question to be addressed in a four-to-five-minute time limit was, "Where are my roots of optimism?" This challenge required deep self-examination. I had no idea how Markus would answer such a subject.

Mr. Chuck, as Markus calls him, arranged a one-night stay for us in South Dakota during the Optimist Club convention. The hotel had a nice stage in the auditorium filled with cushioned seats. I found myself downright emotionally drawn in by the high schoolers and the speeches they presented. One was entirely spoken in American Sign Language as an interpreter verbalized the words. Another referenced hospitals, and I could not help but think he had so much in common with my son. Next, Markus put on the microphone and stepped onto the stage. He set his notecards on the podium and immediately walked to the front, facing everyone.

"Where are my roots of optimism?" Markus enunciated. Each speech was required to originate with this question; otherwise, points would be deducted.

"My life, from the get-go," Markus paused, "has never been ordinary." I kept waiting for the normal raspy gurgle tone to his voice, but no, his speech was clear. He walked across the stage, never taking his eyes off the audience.

"One strong component of my optimism is my connection with people, especially my family and friends. I have a wide circle of support, with these roots stretching from coast to coast and even as far away as England." His right arm was fully extended, followed by his left, with his wide reach naturally demonstrating a great distance.

"My friends and family are the sunshine for my roots. They help hold me in place, to help me re-anchor myself so I don't fall over when chaos comes knocking on the door." He looked so comfortable, more like he was having a personal one-on-one conversation instead of addressing an auditorium of mostly strangers.

"Another source of optimism in my life is music. My choice of music has always been Christian music and very little of anything else." Markus continued. "At times giving up would have been the easier option, but listening to the lyrics of my latest favorite song, 'He is With You,' by Mandisa, is somewhat like 'Eye of the Tiger' to Rocky. It encourages me to focus on what is good and motivates me to stay in the moment. The music helps me to go back to a strong root that I absolutely need: my faith."

Mike sat to my left, tears running down his cheeks. To witness our son—whom we were once told would probably not speak, walk, live—boldly explaining what pushes him through and encourages him to look forward. A lifetime of serious challenges came bubbling up in a single moment. "Brain bleed, enlarged ventricles, possible brain damage . . ."—the memories flashed, but they could not push away the fact that Markus's ability to articulate and do this speech was a gift, a gift that was meant to be shared. The strength, courage, self-assurance—whatever that is with all the challenges he has faced—it was powerful, a pinnacle moment, so unexpected and years in the making.

"I don't know what life has in store for me next. None of us can say for sure, but it is certain that another challenge awaits me in one form or another. With these sources of inspiration, I can face adversity and trust my future will be bright. No matter what happens next," Markus passionately clasped his palms together, "I will cling to what is good. Now and forever."

Markus walked back to the podium to retrieve his notecards. Never once did he so much as glance at them. The microphone was carefully handed back to the moderator as the next teen prepared for their presentation.

Tears blurred my vision, my heart swelling at how beautiful God had made Markus. An immeasurable sense of amazement, with all he had been through, all the could-bes, maybes, not likelys, all the noise in the background during his entire life got quiet. Here was this moment. In four-and-a-half breathtaking minutes, he shared his heart with conviction and confidence. He was not just presenting a speech, but rather speaking the truth.

Mike and I have had front row seats to Markus's whole story. Listening to him share it from padded chairs in the middle of an auditorium, seriously ranks up there with getting married and giving birth.

Any doubts that ever crept in could now take a long hike off a steep cliff. Markus had his athletic scholarship and a scholarship for winning a speech competition. Little could surprise me anymore.

CHAPTER 24
Mom: Class of 2018

Markus's high school graduation (June 2018)

"Mom, we have to pick a date for my grad party," Markus matter-of-factly mentioned as he worked on finishing up his final PSEO classes for high school. A high school degree. Markus is getting a high school degree—a million things simultaneously ran through my mind. I never let myself imagine we would ever see such a regular, yet both somewhat natural and monumental step take place for him. How many times had we been told otherwise, seen the odds stacked a mile high against him? "Mom? Mom?" his voice called to me with increasing volume.

"Yes, Markus, we definitely need to do that," I smiled, my heart so full of gratitude at just the thought. Finding a date was easy. With his older sister Heather working and living in North Dakota, the day before the graduation ceremony made sense. This way she could more easily attend both, an absolute must for Markus.

He surfed the internet for invitation ideas, finding literally thousands and thousands. The Bachman kids had headed out the previous fall with the family camera to shoot some senior photos. They turned out pretty amazing. Markus often does what we lovingly call "school picture faces." His eyes are almost always closed, he looks away, so much like the mischievous comics character Calvin in "Calvin and Hobbes," but not that day. Markus was at his highest weight ever, 135 pounds. Full cheeks, muscles in both arms, and he looked good. Months later he looked his handsome self, even though he was back to a beanpole 115 to 118 pounds. The invite he chose truly displayed his peaceful, content demeanor. The invitation was posted on Facebook, his CaringBridge site, and quite a few were mailed out. This party was officially in motion. We had no clue how many would show up on June 3, but that did not matter. We were celebrating Markus and his most incredible accomplishment yet, surpassing the odds and completing high school.

Canopies were pitched in the backyard, the garage was clean, tables and chairs were in place, and our house had a festive air as did our hearts. Then the guests rolled in, a non-stop flow of constant love from Markus's whole life. He greeted everyone in the driveway as they arrived. It was amazing for me to watch all the wonderful people, remembering the ways each have been involved that ultimately led Markus to this day. Family, friends, healthcare professionals, school professionals, neighbors, classmates; the list goes on. Smiles, laughter, and hugs filled that magnificent afternoon. Our hearts were beyond full.

The next day I watched as Markus put on the light blue graduation gown and cap. He walked into the convention center side room to join all the other 2018 graduates of Bloomington Jefferson High School. I heard the beautiful words loud and clear, "Markus Samuel Bachman," as our son crossed the main stage; the same blue gown fluttered as Markus received his diploma. I wanted to yell, "Do you see this world? He grew up! He persevered!" His enormous smile was so prominent under that mortarboard hat, the tassel swinging with each step. We cheered, clapped wildly, and then those doggone leaky eyes began. But this time, as the dampness rolled slowly down my cheeks, my huge grin matched the one on Markus's face. Oh, my soul, did I ever, ever imagine? And now it was fact. Markus, our Markus, was an official . . . high . . . school . . . graduate. Remarkable.

June 10, 2018 (Markus's post on CaringBridge)
Seven months post-lung surgery, and things are going very well. Thank you, God, for the stretch of health!

Good fun. First and foremost, I have officially FINISHED high school! It's definitely a "woot woot" moment for me and others. It feels a little surreal, but awesome at the same time.

I am thankful that I was healthy for my grad party last Sunday (June 3). Reading through all of the cards, which were filled with words of encouragement, memories, and well wishes, I feel all the more grateful for what I do have, which is the circle of support you all are for me and my family.

I'm so thankful God allowed me to stay healthy so I could attend the high school graduation ceremony last Monday. I was able to walk across the stage to receive my high school diploma, and I'm so grateful for that day.

Markus's high school graduation with Mom and Dad (June 2018)

CHAPTER 25
Heather: Big Sister Chimes In

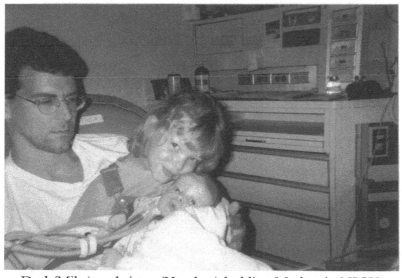

Dad (Mike) and sister (Heather) holding Markus in NICU.
(Summer 1999)

The severity of Markus's medical condition became clear to me when I was a young preteen in late elementary school. As a child, I was consistently exposed to any and all situations, and, whatever it was, it becomes the norm. How was I supposed to know that living with a sibling attached to a ventilation machine wasn't common? You mean, it's not normal that every time an emergency vehicle siren screamed by my school that I automatically associated it, panic-stricken, to something going wrong with my brother? My reality was a baby brother covered in tubes. Our first photo together was taken by an NICU nurse with one of those Polaroid cameras where the pictures develop almost right away. "Bzzzzz," and the camera magically produced the image of us meeting the day he was born. *I did not know* that infants were not supposed to need wires and tubes, or that babies usually wiggle around their crib, and that their cries are not silent.

However, this became my normal. Two months shy of being five years older than Markus, taking on the sister role was a dream come true. A built-in best friend, a partner in crime, a daily pick-me-up, and constant support was the void that my brother ultimately filled in my life. He was MY little brother, and I was his big sister. Then came my second brother, Noah. I love my brothers dearly.

Being the oldest, college came while, in my eyes, they were little. I made the big move from Minnesota to Ohio. Like most high school graduates, I had looked forward to being away from home and beginning a new, independent life on my own. To my surprise, moving thirteen hours away to college in the summer of 2012 was a much harder adjustment than I anticipated. I had envisioned a complete sense of freedom that I deeply craved. It seemed a chance to experience life away from parents, a sibling with specific medical needs, and even my youngest brother, Noah. The summer I left to begin classes and basketball training at Kent State brought a whole new branch of unknowns.

Those thirteen hours away from home meant that I couldn't physically be there for Markus when he was sick, when he was scared, when he was lonely, or when he was isolated. One thing that many people don't consider is the isolation that can go along with a medical condition. Many times, Markus would become confined to our house. He could not go to public places because of the risk of exposure. His energy level would get completely wiped out after a routine weekly subcutaneous immunoglobulin four-needle infusion to boost his immunity. These limitations have forced us to become creative, as no one wants to live in a bubble, so to speak.

My unpredicted daily struggle centered around the guilt that I felt not being there for my younger brother. It pressed extremely heavy on my heart. Ultimately, my at-home life proved more important to me than where I attended school, including the Division One scholarship I had as an ultimate goal. Around the time I chose to transfer to a small private school in Jamestown, North Dakota, Markus's bronchiectasis began to show its unwelcomed horns. His lung started to cause lots of havoc in the middle of his freshman year in high school. In January 2015, Markus had his first lobectomy, the surgery that removed most of his right lung.

Mom and Dad would never let me see Markus right after surgeries and procedures, as most of the time he looked like he got hit by a semi. Bruise-covered arms from the blown IVs, the swollen eyelids from the paralyzing sedation, and the suction running constantly—it's all hard to see. Often I would catch myself wondering what if … "What if I gave Markus one of my lungs? Maybe even one lobe? Would that help Markus or make a difference? What if God, just what if?" The majority of my parents' attention and energy had to go to their sick kid. I get that now. And no, giving him my lung would not fix things, nor was it even an option.

Time passed as Markus went through countless encounters with his life-long doctors, running numerous tests, and trusting that God had a plan through the mess of this all. Dad constantly reminded us to stay in the moment—to stay in the present, every breath, every smile, every tear, every prayer, every moment. I think back to all of those emotions that we so vividly lived. We are human. We fear, we cry, we rejoice, we ache, we beg for peace and comfort, and we talk to God. Those feelings are real, raw, and at times are mind-numbingly intense. After Markus had seemed better for a while, the bloody sputum came back. This time it came back hard. Bronchiectasis is a ruthless disease, merciless as it attacked the vital parts of his remaining right lung, and then began to migrate toward the healthy somewhat-functioning left lung.

Enter lung removal surgery number two. There is no possible way to get comfortable, to rest my eyes in the waiting room. Not just because of the chairs, but because I find myself ironically resisting my own ability to breathe as the surgeons work on regaining Markus's ability to once again inhale and exhale without great effort. The air is tense. I try to not think about the "what ifs" here. The ticking of the clock, as the second hand drags its heels around each passing minute, taunts us as we wait. My parents shoot up at the sound of the door cautiously cracking open, hoping that the operating room nurse or doctor will be there to report encouraging updates. I anxiously clutch the cell phone as it plays through the uplifting Christian music playlist that Markus and I put together. He is specific about the type of music to be played as soon as he transitions into the recovery side of surgery. Knowing how high risk the surgery was, still we fully believed that Markus would be okay, regardless of the outcome. All of these thoughts run laps around my mind while sitting there.

"Oh, God, why now? Please wipe Markus completely clean from the bleeding," I pleaded. As the oldest sibling, I am supposed to protect my younger siblings, to guard them from harm, love them unconditionally, and comfort them when they hurt. But what if I cannot cure what is hurting him? Helpless, yes I felt so helpless the countless times I have watched my thin brother struggle to catch his breath after throwing up over twenty times in one night. How can I protect him when there's NOTHING I can physically do?

Yet there is something: prayer. I physically pray as I reach out my hand toward Markus, breathing with him, for him, as he tries to catch his breath. So many times Markus would be curled over the toilet or in a ball in bed, and we would simply sit with him and pray. The most troublesome part is to be still and know. Be still and know what? God is real. Not some wannabe with selective magical powers. God is capable of hearing even our smallest and David-sized prayers against the Goliath-sized issues in life.

The LORD himself goes before you and will be with you; He will never leave you nor forsake you. Do not be afraid; do not be discouraged.
(Deuteronomy 31:8).

Many people ask how Markus does it. How can Markus be so positive when the life he has been given has been so hard? I believe that Markus maintains his strength, faith, and transparency through a lighthouse type of effect. Lighthouses are meant to withstand the toughest winds and the roughest storms. They do not get wobbly when waters crash around them. They stand there shining. There is no fog so dense, no night so dark, no gale so strong, no mariner so lost but what its beacon light cannot rescue. Markus relies on the lighthouse of the Lord. Enduring faith in His lighthouse builds off of the foundation that keeps Markus grounded, and in turn, keeps us grounded.

CHAPTER 26
Mom: Heart Cath Lab, Again ...

February 2019 (Dad's journal)

❝ ❝ *For the 100th time, the 200th time, I don't even know. My brain aches
and spins. It goes numb. My heart screams out. Put on a brave face for
my family. I'm dying inside. Please God, let it stop. I can't make the
walk back to the operating room and watch him go to sleep one more time.
Your will be done. Not on my strength, but on Yours."*

February 11, 2019 morning (Mom's journal)

Markus is in for his third cardiac cath. Started coughing blood
again. Dang. We had hoped to never see bronchial casts or blood
again.

Mike took him back to the operating room. With a medication
used to relieve surgical anxiety on board, Markus was calm, went
easily to sleep, with no gagging. "Still sucked," Mike wearily said.
His green eyes had that intense concern that oozes sadness.

Now we wait. Will it be fixable? As long as the three of us
have our breath, we will hope. And pray. And wait. Tears have
been close so many times this morning. "I would think eventually
the tears would stop," I quietly told Mike as we made our way to
the family waiting room.

"That's not how we are made," Mike replied as he stared ahead. Very true. We sit in the cardiovascular intensive care unit (CVICU) waiting room for the fourth time. Lost count how many times we have been in the other waiting rooms. Mike and I wait. Maybe I write some words I want in this finished book. Wishing that we could write "and they lived happily ever after," planning that they, meaning us, will.

I hear a doctor talk to a couple on the other side of the barrier. He asked all the questions that we have been asked so many times, things we have been told. One question stopped my heart: "Do your other kids live in a bubble?" asked the doctor. I knew exactly what he meant. In order to protect a medically fragile child, the siblings must live differently in an attempt to limit illness in the home. Their bubble is significantly bigger, but increased limitations become part of their life as well.

"Yes," they answered.

This makes me hope that they can love each other as hard as we do. It is not that awful phrase, "living the dream," it is life—our life. And at times that canvas gets pretty messy, but some of the biggest messes are the most beautiful. One by one, the doctors came out and told us that the procedure went smoothly.

A nurse came into the waiting room. She asked to make a hard copy of Markus's healthcare directive and also for his port-a-cath card. The doctor wants to know if his new port-a-cath is MRI compatible.

This has never happened before. The hospital has a copy of his healthcare directive. Slightly alarmed, I retrieved the paperwork from the medical backpack that is kept in the vicinity of my son. This green camouflage bag is always stocked with items Markus may need: medications, IV supplies, an extra feeding tube, formula, as well as all his vital paperwork, in case of emergency. And then, nurses were talking outside the cardiac room Markus was in before the procedure. They immediately got quiet as I rounded the corner. The looks in their eyes, and the sinking in my guts, confirmed that something bad had happened, something extremely bad.

▶ ▶ ▶ ▶ ▶

On February 11, 2019, the strength in our lighthouse was tested. Markus had gone into Children's Minnesota for what was supposed to be, hoped to be, a same-day procedure. He developed post-surgical obstructive pulmonary edema. His only lung had flooded with fluid.

No one could say whether he would survive the night. No one can ever say or be sure. We arranged for Heather and Noah to come to the hospital, and together we all prayed.

CHAPTER 27
Heather: Stepping in to Write Updates

February 12, 2019, 4:00 a.m.
(Heather's post on CaringBridge)

Big sister here with a long post ahead.
Sitting here writing this, I catch myself attempting to breathe in sync with Markus's vent. The whooshing in and out as he lays still. My ears are more in tune with his pulse as it consistently beeps on the monitor. Mom and I have slept off and on, more off than not. Noah and Dad are in another empty hospital room nearby so they could sleep. Yesterday I almost didn't come home. Mom and Dad are pretty good at being transparent with the state Markus is in, but for this case I wasn't necessarily prepared.

Nothing, and I mean nothing, can prepare you for opening the door to our family home and being told that you and your 12-year-old brother, Noah, need to leave for the hospital right away. The flurry of fear, that sinking feeling in your stomach, and the aching sensation in your chest can be completely consuming and distracting. On my way home from Jamestown, I had an ample amount of time to think. Yesterday morning, I got off work at 7:15 a.m. so I could talk to him before he went back into surgery around 8:30. He had FaceTimed me (video on the phone), and as the sleeping meds started to kick in, I told him I would see him Friday. He did his Markus quirky grin, the one where his bottom teeth go out a little farther in front than his top teeth and blew me multiple air kisses. He said he loved me and see you Friday. This was supposed to be quick.

Getting to the hospital last night at almost 11:00 p.m., that gut-sinking feeling sunk in again. My attempt to remotely keep it together flew out the window. Seeing Mom and Dad wait for us at the bottom of the stairs will be burned forever in my memory. When things like this happen, it's not exactly like what you see in the movies. Although some of the senses are similar in volume, like feeling and hearing your heartbeat pounding in your head, other sounds become muffled, things around you seem to be moving extraordinarily slow, taking baby steps. Markus is a tough guy and the most genuinely pure person I know. Sitting here on this pullout hospital couch, thoughts of us growing up flood around my mind.

His body is still. Analyzing his handsome, grown-up, and shaggy face brings me back to the realization of how far Markus has truly come. I think about us playing together in our toy box after we had dumped out every single toy it held. I think about him letting me put a twirly dress on him along with my denim floral bucket hat and being just as happy as could be. I think about us playing with snow in the bathtub. Mom and Dad brought the snow in when playing outside was too cold for Markus's lungs. I think about him being my built-in best friend, blushing at me even saying a girl's name that he thought was pretty—remembering everything. Through the tears, I know that Markus is resting. But man, do I want my brother back. We have had the chance to do so many things, but there's so much more that I want to experience with him.

I love you Markus and I hope and pray that you'll be reading this entry on Friday, the day that I promised I would be home.

For an update as to his condition, Mom or Dad will be doing that later. Minutes and hours seem long, but each one is precious. As Mom sits by his bedside holding his hand, I encourage you, wherever you are, to reach out a hand as if you were here with us. Take a deep breath, as if you were helping Markus breathe. Each breath is vital, and so is each prayer. The power of prayer is immeasurable. Please keep Markus in your thoughts and prayers, as he needs to be surrounded with healing in this extremely crucial time.

~Heather

We brought the snow inside. (2005)

CHAPTER 28
Mom and Dad: Now Entering Unknown Territory

February 12, 2019, 4:00 p.m.

This is the latest on the post-operative obstructive pulmonary edema:

Lung x-ray this morning showed improvement from twenty-four hours ago. Instead of being entirely "white looking" from the fluid that escaped into his lung, today there are some black patches. Black means air—and not to state the obvious—air in the lung is critical. Blood pressure is better. No blood coming out with suctioning the ventilator tube since 6:00 a.m. The groin used for the cardiac cath looks good. The skin on his tailbone looks good. The vent rate went from thirty-five this morning to a current rate of twenty-six. *This is the type of news we cling to.*

Step one is to try to get the fluid out of the lung as the ventilator maintains pressure on the inside of the lung to control bleeding and fluid leakage. Markus is still heavily sedated on the ventilator. It will be a time of ups and downs as appropriate doses are figured out. Markus has developed a fever and is now receiving antibiotics. The five of us are together in Markus's ICU room.

Thank you for the love and prayers. Very, very grateful to be able to share that Markus is in day two of this latest, unwelcomed development.

~Deb

February 13, 2019

The X-ray this morning looked better than the one yesterday. *We are fans of that trend.*

It has been a constant balancing act with medications to encourage his body to release excess fluid while maintaining hydration, blood pressure, and electrolytes. We are very grateful for how all this is being addressed. The main paralyzing sedation drug was stopped this afternoon. The ventilator rate has been decreased to twenty breaths per minute. I am starting to see yellow on the vent screen, which means that Markus is beginning to take some breaths on his own. He is still heavily sedated.

His situation will be assessed tomorrow, and, if all goes as hoped, it will be time to try to remove the breathing tube (extubate). We are praying that the extra fluid leaves his lung, the bleeding has stopped, and the lung is healthy. In the past, at times when Markus has been extubated, he immediately started singing. Other times it has been rough with vomiting, thick lung secretions, and so on. The singing scenario would be amazing. No matter what comes next, right now it seems like twenty-four hours of moving in the right direction. I hope soon he will be able to write his own update again.

~Deb

February 14, 2019

I'd say it was a fairly quiet day, if getting a PICC line (peripherally inserted central catheter) and having an NG (nasogastric) tube placed can count as quiet. I guess they kind of do, compared to what the beginning of the week looked like.

Before I continue, I have to say something about the presence of God. Through all of you family and friends, through so many staff members here at the hospital who know Markus, through strangers, and even one of Markus's classes at Northwestern are going to pray together tomorrow during class. It's humbling. It lifts us up when we can barely stand on our own. Thank you.

This morning, the initial plan/hope was that Markus would be at a place where the breathing tube could be removed. After considering his chest x-ray, the level of breathing support he was still getting, the types of antibiotics he was on and a couple other things, the notion of removing the breathing tube today "wasn't optimal." Absolutely LOVE his docs, yep, those were the physician's words. With that, we maintained the holding pattern for the most part. And that's fine. As all the staff around here say, "We don't rush Markus. He lets us know when he's ready."

Today did include a couple of notable things. For one, well, when was that last time that you had FOUR IVs running and that WASN'T ENOUGH? Between pain meds, antibiotics, sedation, fluids, diuretic and blood pressure medication (I may have left something out), there was enough incompatibility that he needed all those lines. But then, nutrition got involved. He hasn't received any calories since really early Monday morning. He doesn't have any extra pounds to spare, so he's got to get going on something. With all the anesthesia and narcotics, his GI system shuts down. The nutrition at this point needs to be delivered via IV, which is yet another incompatibility. So this morning, he got a PICC line that is in fact two lines in one. With that, they were able to pull one of the more susceptible lines down by his wrist. So, good and good. It just stinks that they had to poke him again. OK, getting a PICC is NOT just a poke, but there ya go. So now, he's getting some calories again

~Mike

February 15, 2019

Trying not to be anxious.

OK, I wrote that sentence four hours ago as the time to remove the breathing tube was drawing close, and all I could pray was "Please God, let him breathe. Please God."

At 3:00, they stopped the short-acting sedative that kept him fully asleep. At 3:45, the breathing tube came out, and that forty-five-minute span felt like it lasted hours. As he came closer to consciousness, he would cough and wretch and gag. Even with the breathing tube still in, gunk came pouring out of his mouth and they suctioned him constantly. It hurts to see him struggling, and he was working really hard. But the tube came out and stayed out. The lead doc and the anesthesiologist who was on standby both agreed within the first ten minutes that "he looks good." And then they asked us what we thought. Uuuhhhh, so once we/I could think for a second and find words, we agreed. It was the right time with the right people. But mostly, Markus's body said it was right. And yes, he looked good. He was breathing with no tube down his throat.

And now it's after 8:00 p.m. He's at a sedation level where he's between fuzzy and asleep. He's clearing a ton of junk from his lung. It's constant. It's hard to believe there can be that much crud in there. And early on, there was some bright-ish blood. NO! No blood! No more! Ever! Was it caused by irritation from the breathing tube, or was it old stuff that had settled beyond the reach of the suction? Don't know for sure, and don't care. DON'T WANT TO SEE ANY MORE OF IT. The docs were okay with the amount for now and said to just monitor it, trusting it isn't active bleeding in the lung. We're trusting that, too.

Now's a very busy time with coughing, clearing, and suctioning. It's also a tricky time because Markus is trying really hard to be awake, trying to communicate either through motioning or signing/finger spelling. Yes, even in a semi-conscious state, he wants to talk. And for the most part, it just doesn't work. We know that the tube in his nose bugs him. I'm sure we don't have his Bi-PAP mask on quite right, and it's uncomfortable. We know he really doesn't like the urinary catheter. And on top of that, he wants to know everything about what's happened and what's going on. He's Markus. But there will be the right time to go over all that's happened. Maybe tomorrow as the sedation gets lighter and he becomes more awake, or maybe the next day.

We are just grateful there is a today. Thankful for you all.
~Mike

CHAPTER 29
Mom: "Please Come Back"

The day after the ventilator was removed was a transitional day. A necessary evil, full of pain, clearing lung junk, and puking. Then hallucinations began. Markus was convinced slimy black creatures clung to his legs. To him, they were 100 percent real. His dad removed invisible leeches from Markus's thighs and threw them in the trash. Without fear or distress, Markus also believed he had died. His spoken words were calm, heartfelt, almost otherworldly: "Dad, you and Mom should adopt another child to replace me," Markus shared in a peaceful tone.

His dad was stunned. How could Markus even think that way? "There is no way we could ever replace you, son," he answered. "Do you want to come back?"

Markus's eyes shot wide open, asking, "It's *not too late* to come back?"

"No, it's not too late. Do you want to come back right now?" replied his dad.

"Yes, there are things I need to fix and finish." What an odd statement coming from one of the kindest, honest, purest people we have ever encountered. Yet, Markus shared how everything he had ever done wrong had been exposed to him.

For five days, our extremely logical son hallucinated and spoke of things yet to come. The confusion and disconnect terrified us. His brain completely altered into a Markus that we had never met.

Part of us was afraid that he would be stuck like that. At times, his face shone like a little child's on Christmas morning, and such was the case one morning as he dug through his blankets in search of the puppies that shared the bed with him. "Don't you see their cute, little black faces, Mom?" Markus asked, with joy and adoration smeared over his entire face.

"No, Markus, I am sorry, I do not see any puppies," I answered. I shook each piece of bedding out one by one and ran my hand over the bottom sheet. "Please believe us. We would not lie to you."

February 20, 2019 (Mom's post on CaringBridge)
Any medical professional who has ever worked with Markus knows that he is cautious and super protective of his IV lines. Anyone who touches them is under his watchful guard. Tug it ever so slightly, and you will definitely hear about it. At four this morning, I was told he had started to remove his own PICC dressing. I knew then that his mind still was not clear. I stayed up after that and watched him sleep. He would sit up, reach around like he was working on something, constantly rubbing his thumb and pointer finger. Honestly, I was getting a little annoyed because his brain so badly needs rest. Around 5:30 a.m. Markus refused to close his eyes anymore. He calmly talked of things so real and yet so distant, I had to struggle to keep myself together.
    (End of post)

"Mom, you need to let me go. I love you and appreciate all you have done for me, but I need to go," Markus said as he kissed my cheek and held my hands. Gratitude filled his eyes as they locked on mine.

"It is okay." He threw off his blankets and swung his feet over the hospital bed railing.

"I do not think this is how it works, Markus, but here is the truth. You are God's child. We love you with everything that is in us and always will love you," I told him. Markus seemed so sure that he was leaving. His face was bright and confident. At that moment, he was persistent that I needed to release him.

Raising a child like Markus has taught us that anything is possible with God. Could this be our last goodbye? Maybe, but most likely not. I could recall only two stories in the Bible that spoke of two men, Elijah and Enoch, being taken straight from earth to heaven.

I buzzed for his nurse to walk with him. This short, dark-haired nurse had never met Markus until that morning. "Maybe this is his new normal," she commented as we assisted Markus safely out of bed.

"No. NO, NO, NO!" my brain screamed. "No, Lord, you can bring him back," I prayed. I could not imagine my logical, thoughtful son living so disconnected from this world, from us. Listening and seeing him so cognitively altered crushed my heart in a way I never had experienced before.

Markus continued glancing back at me as he walked with the new nurse. Thankfulness and love filled his eyes in what he believed were our final glimpses of each other on this earth. With a silent prayer, I released my son. "He is yours, Father, Thy will be done." Markus stopped walking. Confusion on his face, his eyes darted around the room. In them, I recognized a glimmer of my son as he reached for the doorframe.

"Ugh, I feel a little dizzy," he said in a stronger voice, his voice.

Shortly after that, the ICU physician and a pulmonologist came in to talk. "Markus, are you tired of fighting?" asked the ICU doctor. She had earlier shared with me that she had seen patients have similar premonitions and visions before they died.

Markus explained that he felt as though he was going between worlds. Calmly he answered, *"But I am not ready to give up."* That afternoon, he was given an MRI to determine if something like an air bubble or a cardiac coil had migrated to his brain and caused these cognitive changes. Such relief to learn the scan was normal!

That same evening, Markus was sound asleep by 7:30 p.m. Finally. We welcomed his time of rest with open arms.

CHAPTER 30
Dad: A Father's Whisper

I welcome the stillness.

Quiet. Except for the small cracklings of bones in my spine as muscles release their rigid hold. Inhale, exhale, focus, release the tension. My oldest son's body finally laid still, at rest, his long limbs stretching out in the almost-too-short pediatric hospital bed. For now, I allow exhaustion to sink in and my thoughts to wander.

Importance of being intentional

Markus's demands on my time have been extensive, so much greater than normal. Because of that, my ability to be there for my other kids has not been what I hoped or wanted. Both Heather and Noah reached ages where they were able to "process" and understand the "why"—why I sometimes had to spend a disproportionate amount of time with Markus. Before that time, though, it was just unfair to them. They were regular little kids who wanted attention from their dad, to proudly show him what they made at school, to play, to have him tuck them in, to hold them. I had spent many days away from them when Markus's condition was very poor. All I could offer my other kids at those difficult times was a wavering, tearful voice on the phone. Trying to force my voice to be steady as I told them, "I love you. I miss you so much." Never would I have anticipated such pain coming simultaneously from multiple directions, but so often it did.

162 . MARKUS BACHMAN AND DEB BACHMAN

At other times though, and with nearly the same intensity, occasions would come when I could just be with my kids. I was able to fully experience with them what they were doing at the time. I could see and hear them perform. I could watch them present. I could smile at them, and they could see me there. I could play with them, hear and feel them laugh, watch them grow, and hug and congratulate them. It's those moments that burned so much more brightly, so much more intensely. And what I came to realize was this was only possible because I was truly present. I was so very intentional about being present, paying attention, being in the moment with that child, and loving them the best I could. That was the key. I'm so thankful my eyes were opened to how valuable and how rich life can be by being present, even under our circumstances.

Now my focus is back to Markus
What version of Markus will return to us? The one we know? Someone completely different? Will his mind be affected? How will our delicate life balance be impacted? How in the world would our family manage this on top of all the physical demands of his medical needs? EXHALE. "Stay in the moment," I whisper to myself. *Don't borrow the worries of tomorrow as today has enough worries of its own.* For this instant in time, Markus is quiet. I quiet myself, my exhausted mind. I stay in the moment.

Then in the quiet, ever so briefly, my mind is no longer intensely focused on him. It wanders off for just a minute to ponder my work. I have an obligation to my employer. They pay me to contribute. I am positive that most other workplaces would have dismissed me time and time again. Over and over, I am humbled by the depth of compassion I have been offered by my coworkers and the flexibility afforded by my superiors. They allow me to fully focus on Markus when I've needed to be at the hospital to support Markus and my wife. I have been allowed to melt into lostness, if needed. I've been allowed to gradually ramp up my work tasks as I was able, but then given the latitude to step away in an instant again if his condition got worse. I have been so, *so* blessed to work *for* such understanding people, to work *with* such understanding people. Thankfully, my job does not weigh heavily on my heart as I sit with my sleeping Markus.

In this lull, I have allowed myself to ponder these things that life has become. Suddenly, I'm jarred back into the present. Whether one of his machines alarmed or a nurse walked in, he coughed or moved, I don't recall. But now I am back to my groanings, asking "please." I'm not even sure what "please" is asking for, but God does. I don't have to know nor, at this point, am I even capable of knowing. Perhaps it's asking for Markus's mind to be restored. Perhaps I'm asking that his health be restored. Or maybe I'm asking that his life be spared. Instead, I might be asking that God prepare me for what is to come. Such is life with Markus—filled with intense, emotional questions, ones that we don't even know what we're asking and certainly don't know the answers to.

My thoughts are focused on my family. For now, I soak in the quiet, confident the five of us will love each other through whatever we must face.

Once again, softly I ask, "Oh, God, please," as I have pleaded so many times in the past, now facing something totally new, "please bring back my son."

CHAPTER 31
Heather: Time to Rejoice

Markus and Heather (2019)

March 1, 2019 (Heather's post on CaringBridge)

Last night when I arrived back home again, the greeting at the bottom of the stairs was much, much, *much* different. At the base of our basement stairs stood a familiar face. This time my heart didn't sink, but swelled with an overwhelming amount of relief. With a big sigh and a squeal of his hearing aid being too close, I could hug Markus again. My brother Markus was fully back and only two pounds skinnier than prior to the surgery almost three Mondays ago. For those who know me, I'm a hugger, so being able to embrace Markus again after the whirlwind of those few weeks was nothing short of a God-given miracle. Hugging him, the real Markus, was all I could think about last Friday when I had to go back to North Dakota to work a long weekend at my job. Some days it's hard working with medically fragile kids like ours at the center, especially when some cases hit so close to home. When I look at the kids I work with, parts of each of them remind me of Markus. They share many similarities: some of their conditions, their personalities, their surgeries, their treatments, and their likes/dislikes. Working with the medically fragile kids as I do, constantly validates that this is the field in which I know I'm meant to work. I feel for these children's families, and I can't imagine what it must be like not to have your child living at home with you. Over two weeks in the hospital is long enough for us.

So if you could, add to your prayer list healing and comfort for the kids at the center. Many have gone through more than most of us combined will ever have to face. Pray for their families, as I cannot imagine how hard it would be to be so far away from your loved one, knowing most will never come back home. Pray for peace for the families, our physician, our nurse practitioners, nurses, and direct support professionals who day in and day out care for these kids. Yes, it does take an army.

This morning Mom and I went to the University of North-western in St. Paul with Markus. And no, we did not sit in class with him. (Having your mom and older sister there, how embarrassing!) Instead Mom and I bought a bagel, sat, and talked. It's rare for the two of us to have time. It was almost surreal because it was the first time I had gone to college with Markus and realized that my brother was attending a real and normal college. Sounds silly, but sometimes parts of life randomly sneak up on you. I'm continually humbled by the experiences my family and I have been given the opportunity to witness. Although it may seem simple and insignificant, I got to take Markus to school today.

Tonight we sat at the dinner table, all six of us—Mom, Dad, Noah, Markus, me, and Grandma. It felt good to laugh. It felt good to know that I can still be embarrassing to Noah. It felt so incredibly good to look over and see Markus there with his chin resting on his hand, and it felt good to pray. While Dad was praying, I couldn't help but to look around. You know how little kids do when they peek one eye open during a prayer? I'll admit that was me tonight. All too real was a rush of undivided peace and pure joy. My family was back together, under the roof where our parents raised and continue to raise us three kids. My parents have defied the odds when it comes to divorce rates while having a child with medical needs. Seeing them function as a team, making it a priority every morning to embrace and hug each other, turning to God to strengthen them to together lead by example, and truthfully being transparent when life might show its not-so-pretty colors—this is what makes my parents one of a kind.

Quick story about them.

We spent Valentine's Day at the hospital, as Markus remained on the vent and was paralyzed that day. Mom, Dad, and I were there with Markus, and the Ronald McDonald House was putting on a dinner as they do almost every night of the week. My parents were completely tunnel-vision focused on Markus and his needs. For those who know my parents, well, you can about imagine. At this point, at least one of us was always at Markus's bedside. On Valentine's Day, the nurse and I told my parents to go eat dinner together. Now this may seem like a little thing, but Dad took Mom's hand, did a dorky laugh, smiled, and skipped in place like a little boy would do. I heard Mom laugh, an authentic laugh. And down two flights of stairs to the Ronald McDonald House they went. Things like that make me realize how lucky my brothers and I are not only to have parents who love us unconditionally but also who sincerely love each other unconditionally and live out their wedding vows to this day—which brings me back to my point of laughter.

Yes, laughter is the best medicine. Dad thanked God for laughter tonight, and boy, thank GOODNESS for laughter. Hearing Markus giggle-snort and Noah squeak-laugh, my heart is full. For tonight, I'm staying in the moment. Even if that means I have to sleep on an air mattress underneath Markus's mounted deer head with Christmas lights threaded through the antlers.

~Heather

(End of post)

When I look at my family, friends, the kids I work with, whomever I may encounter, I try to take a second to really notice them. Growing up with Markus taught me this. I see the color in his eyes, his perfectly imperfect smile, his slightly slumped right shoulder, and his scrunched nose as he belly laughs to the point of tears. I ultimately realized that having Markus as a sibling was everything short of typical. He was and continues to go against "the norm," but in ways far greater than any of us could have imagined. The all-out pursuing of his dreams, exceeding in classes in his Markus way, his brain always so filled with a work ethic unlike anyone else that I have met. It makes me want to yell, "God is so good, ya'll! I mean, have you met my brother?" If not, you are truly missing out on one of the best experiences this world has to offer. I am not saying this because he is my brother. Truth is, this guy is flat out one amazing human. And gratefully, his story continues.

CHAPTER 32
Mom: Reflecting

Family photo at Villard (2018)

Shaggy whiskers cover Markus's dimpled chin. An organizational planner sits open on his desk. Next to the unchecked boxes lies a thick quantum analysis book, displaying pages of tiny print. And yet, somehow, a contagious boyish excitement still radiates in his smile. He is years from the fragile infant in the NICU, decades beyond our initial "Please give him a chance." The answer to that prayer has taken our lives on a route we never imagined or knew existed.

Along this unforeseen path, we have witnessed unimaginable generosity, kindness, and love. I have seen my husband humbly lead and unite our family through harrowing months of uncertainty. I have experienced the beauty of forgiveness as we, especially me, repeatedly fall short. The struggles are real. What has his survival cost our family? Freedom to travel anywhere we choose? The ability to up and do anything active we desire? Quiet nights where death is not a regular part of daily thoughts for each of us? Privacy in our own home? Financially?

Yes, there has been a cost, but anything negative is completely overshadowed by his beautiful life. This remarkable drama has shown us firsthand that God is always there for us, even when life looks different than we think it should. Markus grew up in an imperfect world with imperfect parents under often-challenging circumstances. To us, he is a priceless gift.

CHAPTER 33
Markus: The Bottom Line at Twenty

Summer 2019

M y story could have ended so differently so many times. Statistically speaking, I should be belly up in a grave. The delivery room should have been both my entrance and exit to this world, but here I am, twenty years of life here on earth. *I am 20 years old!*

That first medical article my mom read stated that there was a 97 percent mortality rate for infants born with an LTE type IV cleft. Those are not very favorable odds in such a circumstance, and perhaps it is the actual reason I do not personally give much weight to certain human predictions. We like to think we are oh-so-smart and in charge, but I know who is truly in control. It is in Him I place my trust.

My first year as a full-time college student recently came to a close. It was literally surreal finishing that last final of the 2019 spring semester. I am completely grateful to have made it back to a classroom, and I have enjoyed every moment. I officially declared accounting as my major because pursuing this degree fits me well.

I also started my first job as a teaching assistant at the University of Northwestern in St. Paul. How awesome is that? The day I was officially offered the position I was over the moon with joy. For the first time in my life, I have a job I can do that is a good fit regarding my health situation. I work as much as my health will allow. Being an academic coach for other students feels quite natural for me. Practical strategies I have learned from missing classes and long breaks from my studies are most helpful to other students as we discuss their academic challenges. I truly have been blessed to have so many amazing people guiding, supporting, and loving me. Now it is my turn to give back. On the days I do not have students to coach, there are plenty of projects to keep me productive, such as converting paper files into a digital database. I really like what I am doing; it gives me a good mix and is never monotonous.

There is always opportunity to throw some fun in the mix with college and working. Bowling, fishing, searching for cars with my Uncle Ed, playing games with friends and family, reading; I could go on and on. Bonus blessings like these make life extra sweet, especially when things get heavy.

Health challenges continue, and honestly, I am not a fan of a couple of life issues I faced this summer. It was supposed to be a summer break filled with work and one class. Three consecutive weeks of unfortunate cyclic vomiting episodes, including excruciating headaches, puking at least seventy-five times, and losing more precious weight—all are seriously draining me. Coughing out blood to the tune of two emergency room visits and a current hospitalization make me feel like the IV medications will never end. Once again, incredibly, the medications are helping improve my health.

Today I start something new: a drug, along with counseling to help deal with unwelcomed anxiety that has ballooned within me. A compassionate lung doctor told me last month, as I cried uncontrollably in the hospital, that they would be concerned I was delusional or in denial (or even had a pulse) if I did not respond with emotion to everything that was happening. What a massive, internal relief it was, being told *that I am normal and human*! I'm trusting that the ping-ponging thoughts that have kept me awake lately will take a hike. Enough already!

Despite all the challenges my health still presents, I definitely have hopes for my future. I plan to graduate college with my accounting degree and then possibly pursue a certification as a certified public accountant (CPA). Until recently, a career in the automotive world remained my professional goal. I read car magazines cover to cover, and three of my letters to the editor have appeared in *Car and Driver* magazine. Even though I have always really enjoyed cars, I am sensing that my career will lead me down a different path. For that reason, I am keeping all options open.

Someday, maybe, I will get married, but only if that is part of the plan for my life here on earth. I am in no hurry, and I am trusting God will make it quite evident if I am to take that step. I have yet to go on a date, but again, I am in no rush. When the right person comes along, I think it will be obvious. If marriage is in my cards, perhaps someday I will have children, but right now I am on the fence with that one. No pressure intended, Heather and Noah, but it would be flat-out incredible, talking future here, to wear the title Uncle Markus.

I have a definite passion for the country atmosphere. Give me green space, trees, and lakes any day. Truth be told, I am not a white-knuckle, rush-hour kind of guy. Passing the occasional rusty pickup truck on a peaceful two-lane county road is more my speed. Living in a small town would be ideal for this city guy.

God willing, I hope to grow old, with gray hair and wrinkled skin, the whole deal. I think we all truly would like that. In my eyes, aging is a gift to be cherished.

Most importantly, I do not ever want to lose sight of what is most important. To me, that means relationships with people. *Stuff truly does not matter; people do.* The wise words of my current 20-year-old self, perhaps the future 30-year-old me may have a different answer, but I hope not. It is astonishing how this singular truth is so not shiny, but rather plain, simple, and beautiful. I hope to stash this priority in my back pocket, taking it on every detour and back road this life of mine travels.

To be sure I never forget, I am adding something else to my back-pocket list: *I am human.* This is a thought worth embracing. I am human, which is okay. In fact, one evening in the hospital, a family friend recommended I read Psalm 103. I read it a couple of times, kinda got the gist of it, but it did not totally sink in. It was getting late, and I wanted to put down my Bible to go to sleep. For some reason, I could not yet let go of my Bible for the night. In fact I could not let it go physically. An urge, a sense, a small invisible voice—I do not know how to describe it exactly—told me to find a certain passage. All I knew was that it was in the New Testament, but did not know which book, chapter, let alone verse. I started reading the headings and flipping through the New Testament. In *John 9:1-7*, it felt like it jumped off the page and slapped me in the face.

John 9:1-7 JESUS HEALS A MAN BORN BLIND.

As he went along, he saw a man blind from birth. His disciples asked him, "Rabbi, who sinned, this man or his parents, that he was born blind?"

"Neither this man nor his parents sinned," said Jesus, "but this happened so that the work of God might be displayed in his life. As long as it is day, we must do the work of him who sent me. Night is coming, when no one can work. While I am in the world, I am the light of the world."

Having said this, he spit on the ground, made some mud with the saliva, and put it on the man's eyes. "Go," he told him, "wash in the Pool of Siloam." So the man went and washed, and came home seeing.

That night in the hospital, it was weird in the moment. As I read and reread this passage quite a few times, it truly changed my perspective of what was happening to me. I had become so frustrated, so tired of this constant cycle of health issues. I was losing what it felt like to feel healthy and not need an IV.

Now I am thankful that I imploded the way that I did. I had reached a breaking point, and now finally I was able to deal with and manage the anxiety and frustration that had increasingly wreaked havoc. The words, *"This happened so that the work of God might be displayed in his life,"* are now burned in the back of my mind. No matter what comes, I know this will help as I face each new or recurring situation. They were the words I desperately needed at that time, as well as providing a message that has rearranged my thinking. It helped reshape what was going on and gave me reassurance. Jesus may not come to me today, rub mud on my chest, and heal me, but I know He is in this with me, even when I do not completely understand. And that is okay.

Would I like to be 100 percent healed? Of course, and I will keep asking and trusting God for that. Most important though, is *His will be done on earth as it is in heaven.*

CHAPTER 34
Markus: Gratitude

November 2, 2019 (Markus's post on Facebook)

November 2 may be a normal day for most people, but in my family, November 2 marks some events we will not forget, even if I don't remember the events very well.

On November 2, 1999, I came home for the first time after spending the first five months of my life at Children's Minnesota Hospital.

November 2, 2007, I had my trach tube removed. The remaining hole in my throat was surgically closed in February 2008.

November 2, 2017, I got my driver's license *and* bowled my highest personal three-game best series (with individual game scores of 213, 228, and 194 for a 635 total series), both on the same day.

Today, November 2, 2019, marks twenty years since I came home from the hospital for the first time.

Life hasn't always been easy. It has had its up-and-down periods, but my heart is full of gratefulness.

Thank you, Mom and Dad, for all that you have both done and what you continue to do to help me. Thank you for allowing the doctors to do the surgeries on me the day I was born, even though the odds seemed to be stacked against me.

Thank you, Heather, for being there for Noah and me—for the times where we have smiled and had fun, for when you have come home immediately when things haven't gone well for me, and for everything in between.

To all my other family members and friends, thank you all for your support, prayers, visits, love, etc. Thank you for how you have helped my family out time and time again. On behalf of my family, thank you.

To all the medical people, thank you for all you have done and continue to do, to help me maintain my health. Thank you for being there to help me (and my family) through the valleys of my life.

Most importantly, though, is that I'm thankful to God for giving me faith, endurance, and hope. Without Him, I wouldn't be who I am today.

Despite my challenges, I strive to live life to the fullest. As a tire cover on the back of a Hummer vehicle I saw said, "1 Life Live It." I have my continual struggles, but I choose not to let them define who I am. My challenges will not stop me.

▶ ▶ ▶ ▶ ▶

To be open about this, it has been three years since I first received that old blue binder filled with emails. Honestly, I could handle reading only a few pages. Those details, my history, were too much for me to process. Instead, I choose to live the days I have been given the best I can, one breath at a time, cherishing this precious gift called life.

Markus and his lifelong pulmonologist, Dr. Pryor (2008)

Minnesota Twins game with the grandparents (2013)

Dad, Markus, Heather, Mom, and Noah (March 2020)

ADDENDUMS

Protectors of Health: Yes, a Runny Nose Can Be a Serious Health Threat

U nknown to us, we fell under the category of "watchmen" the day Markus was born. We became sentinels standing guard to defend our guy against germs. What causes a slightly irritating runny nose, tiny cough, or scratchy throat in one person can land Markus in the hospital for weeks. Mike and I have to divide our time. One stays by Markus's side and the other cares for our other kids, addressing only the duties that are the bare minimum to our regular life. Since Mike is our main breadwinner, I am usually the one with Markus as Mike does his best to work and do everything else. More importantly, Markus becomes extremely, even dangerously, sick. Due to the seriousness of the ramifications, we have had to be, and still are, overly cautious about risking health exposure, especially in our home.

People with any cold symptoms, even the slightest tickle, are not allowed inside our house. Often, especially in the winter, we avoid exposure to someone who is in close contact with another person currently experiencing symptoms. No one wants to live this way, *but we have to.* Everywhere we go, everything we do, is first scrutinized by the question: Is this safe for Markus? When visitors to our home pass the health inspection, they must unknowingly endure the "sniff" test. Any strong smells? Perfumes?

Animals/pets? Cigarette smoke? Home has to be his safe zone, protected in the best, humanly way possible. Under normal circumstances, a minor illness would not matter, but in our world, it could be a life-threatening exposure.

The place this gets the trickiest is with family. For us, extended family has always been an important part of our lives. Larger groups, for us, means lots of fun and time making memories together. However, big groups also increase the risk of exposure to a greater number of pathogens. Mike and I had to, and continue to, make decisions based on whether or not we believe an event or visit is safe for Markus. Is it our desire to be social? Absolutely. No one chooses to be limited and isolated, but our son cannot afford for us to be reckless. Honestly, we are the ones deferring or canceling nine out of ten times because our kid is not well, or while looking at the big picture, we decide that the activity is not feasible. It is incredibly painful on that rare day the stars align, it looks like we can participate, and then someone shows up with a cough or runny nose.

What do we do now? Please, I do not want to have this conversation one more time. This topic repeatedly causes us physical and emotional pain. Our struggles are not transparent to those who do not spend hours caring for our son. We get that, but trust those of us who witness the fallout firsthand.

Public gatherings are another story. Being outdoors is our preferred choice. Larger, enclosed spaces, like the bowling alley or church, are places we try to go because those activities bring Markus a lot of joy. At all times, we are intensely aware of our surroundings, constantly listening for coughing, looking for watery, tired eyes, or red, irritated noses that show the evidence of an illness. At a movie theater or church, if one person coughs, we move to another part of the room. If we hear peppered coughing, we leave. This will not change.

Attending school is Markus's absolute favorite thing to do. So, with the help of others, we put every possible plan into action to make this possible. *Choosing to enjoy this adventure called life, albeit in a unique way, is something Markus does quite well.* I believe we have our "village" to thank for that. You are exceptional. We fully know that to choose to be in our lives requires a whole different level of "stick with it," especially now that this lifestyle has gone on for two decades.

If you know or meet a family with similar health concerns, it may help to keep the following in mind:

1. **If someone has a child who spent time in a neonatal intensive care unit (NICU), the family will need to be careful long after the baby has been discharged from the hospital.**

Being vigilant may be their necessary new normal. Not everyone is willing to maintain a friendship that has lost freedoms that were once part of the relationship. If you choose to stand with the family, it will take a different level of acceptance and understanding on your part. Our lives changed dramatically after Markus was born, as did a number of our relationships. *Those who chose to stay by our side all these years are priceless treasures.*

2. **A proactive attitude is necessary to help the parents protect their child.**

It gets very old hearing the phone ring the evening before a social gathering. "So and so has symptom X, do you think that would be a problem?" If you even have to ask the question, it is probably not okay. Do not make the parent always say no or miss the event. "It is just allergies," is another statement we often hear. It may well be allergies, but we cannot be 100 percent sure of that and, even so, if someone has discharge from the nose, it's guaranteed there are germs in that snot being blown and sneezed out. We had to take our youngest, Noah, to an allergist to figure out what he was allergic to, and how we could best help Noah manage his symptoms.

Because we have to bow out so frequently, please give us the chance to leave our home and be social. You do not want to miss the event or party? We totally understand how you feel. Our lives changing completely may also have changed yours. Together, we can figure this out without risking our child ending up in the hospital. Your diligence helps us stay sane and upright on two feet. *We appreciate it more than words can express.*

3. Please wash your hands often, without complaining.

If we have hand sanitizer out, please use it. Friends of Heather, Markus and Noah, from a young age, learned that the first thing they do at our house is wash their hands. They wash again after eating or using the bathroom. We are not germaphobes, but we are bona fide "germ aware." WE HAVE TO BE PRO-ACTIVE, scouting everything like hawks. This will not change. *Please respect this vital Bachman house rule.*

4. Accept that our energy is very limited—and must be preserved.

With that being said, we also need other people in our life. I may not call you back as quickly as I had in the past. Please forgive me. I have to make so many calls each day along with everything else. Medical calls, insurance difficulties, and arranging necessary additional help are mind numbing. And somewhere deep inside lurks a nagging little voice that taunts, "How are you ever going to get through this?" I have learned to tell that negative voice to shut up, then move on to deal with each need, one moment at a time, one issue at a time. Some days it is easier to do than others. Most families are truly doing the best that they can. If that is what you are seeing, tell them. Yours may be the words that help during the next stressful episode.

To those of you who choose to be pillars of our village, we are forever grateful. To those whose lives move in a different direction, we are thankful for how our paths once crossed.

THANKS TO YOU AND YOU...YOUR HELP WAS A GAME CHANGER

I have heard two statements over and over, and most days I do not have a clear-cut, decisive answer. "Call if you need anything" usually leaves me completely tongue-tied. "How can I help?" makes my mind feel like it is immediately an empty, blank void. It is both humbling and wonderful when others want to help. We need help, lots of help, more than I will ever admit.

We have been blessed by the love and support of others. Many have reached out to our family in a variety of ways, some listed below—and you can do the same for people you know in need of help.

CHILDCARE

Still pregnant and newly admitted to Abbott Northwestern Hospital, my parents brought 4-year-old Heather to visit me. My dad held my hand while telling me, "Do not worry about Heather. We will keep her as long as you need. This baby needs you the most right now." Anyone caring for my healthy children during one of our many crises is priceless. Visiting with all my kids during times of calm makes beautiful memories. My parents visited us every Friday, staying until after supper. Without being asked, my mom sometimes had packed a bag and stayed if we needed more help. My parents and a neighbor gave us permission to call at all hours. They never made us feel like a burden and did not put time limits on their availability. Over the years, Markus's grandparents developed their own health issues. My sister and brother-in-law, our neighbors, and then a wonderful family from church, willingly stepped into that role for our youngest, Noah. In our circumstances, these people are definitely "game changers," not only for us as parents, but even more so for our kids.

People that have been comfortable enough to learn how to handle Markus's medical care are our lifeblood. Although we really wanted to, Mike and I could not, and still cannot, care for our son alone 24/7. Truly, all I wanted to do was take care of my kids without needing other people in our home to help with Markus. In addition to his daily medical care, I was exhausted from dealing with numerous insurance appeals. After yet another health insurance denial stating that homecare nursing was "not medically necessary," I was out of energy to address again how Markus does not neatly fit into any established healthcare categories. Defeated and yet determined, we tried it solo. Within two months I was sidelined with constant migraines. It is a fact: Human beings require more than two hours of sleep each day. Homecare professionals re-entered our life and continue to assist our family even today. We remain hopeful that one day Markus will be able to do all his medical care on his own.

ANIMALS
Taking our dog the entire time Markus was in the hospital was a gift some families have given us. Those who cared for Markus's beloved rabbits and dog gave him peace of mind so he could focus on recovery. Pets are work. It is an immense relief to know that our furry friends are well cared for while we, as parents, focus on our kids.

HOME MAINTENANCE

The snow piles up, the grass keeps growing, and leaves fall no matter what tragedy pops up. Mail is delivered daily, and the garbage needs to be brought to the curb once each week. Sometimes we do not even know whom to thank for taking care of these tasks. We hope you know how grateful we are *for the gift of time you gave us.*

FOOD

I did not realize how much energy cooking took until my reserves were on empty. The dinners that people have delivered have refueled our bodies so often. Meals every night would have been too much. Two prepared meals a week would nourish our bodies for four nights, and that really bolstered our spirits. It is a rare form of tasty encouragement. When I was in the hospital for a month, one family kept the refrigerator in my room stocked for Mike. My husband was trying to work his full-time job, spend time with Heather at my parents, visit me in the hospital, all the while knowing that we would be having a new baby any minute. The delivered food and the love it represented gave him much-needed energy to persevere.

ROAD TRIPS AND SOCIAL EVENTS

The fun stuff can get tricky. We enjoy adventure and travel, but there is a different level to packing and planning when a person has medical needs. The demands of a healthcare regimen do not go away because one chooses to vacation. My brother has willingly given whole weekends to assist his nephew on overnight hunting excursions. Helping families get creative about spending a few nights out of the house is priceless. For Markus, these opportunities have led to new lifelong passions.

CHILDHOOD FRIENDSHIPS

We all need at least one friend. Friendships cannot be forced, but they can be encouraged. A little girl in our neighborhood added such fun and spark to Markus's life. They spent hours together doing all sorts of fun kid things like playing board games, drawing, and creating all types of business plans. She patiently would sit next to Markus when he got treatments or struggled with his health. Often, Markus vomited. This little girl would just wait for it to be cleaned up and then go on as if this were just a regular thing. Many children will not wait for a child that cannot "keep up." Those who do, or are taught to, are some of the most amazing individuals I have ever met.

FINANCIALLY

This was the most humbling and difficult for Mike and me. We like to picture ourselves as independent, capable adults. Two weeks before the trip to Texas for Markus's lung transplant evaluation, random checks arrived in our mailbox out of the blue. It was a very uneasy time for us all, and these unexpected hugs reminded us that we were not alone in this. Some friends have hosted events that donated proceeds to our family. Every time it looked like we were going to start going under financially, something surprising, quite startling, showed up. We are in a better financial place now, but at times in the past, it was a different story.

Having a child with health issues can add tremendously to family expenses—much more than most families would ever openly share.

EMPLOYMENT

We know that we are extremely blessed with the companies that have employed Mike. They allowed him flexible hours and the ability to work from his computer at the hospital. We did all we could so that our home life did not interfere with Mike's work, but no parent can focus and give their undivided best if their child is extremely sick. My husband's employers understood this and have been flexible. Mike's job carries the health insurance—and this has to remain a top priority for us despite what is happening in our personal lives.

After my graduation in 2005, I put my registered nurse license to use part-time for a few years. Unfortunately, our reality reached a point that made me too unreliable. Someday I hope to work again as a nurse.

When Markus was not yet a year old, I was asked to speak at the Minnesota capitol regarding highly skilled in-home nursing. However, in the end, my testimony was not required to protect this vital service. For some reason, I felt led to attend the session even though I would not be speaking. As I sat in the audience facing our state representatives, I listened to other parents share their lives. An older, gray-haired man walked up to the microphone. He and his wife had been caring for their only child for over twenty years. She required a wheelchair and full assistance. This father shared how he often had to miss work when his daughter was hospitalized or because his wife had injured her back lifting their adult child. The multiple absences were mentioned on many of his annual performance reviews, and he was not promoted. He does not know this, but I still hear his closing words to this very day: "Most parents fear their child passing away before them. When you have a child like mine, you fear your own death happens before your son or daughter, because who in the world will step in to care for them?"

CARINGBRIDGE

CaringBridge is referenced numerous times in Markus's story. It is an invaluable resource that conserves our time and emotional reserves. Individually verbalizing medical updates over and over when Markus is in the hospital can be draining. We do our best to post frequent updates on his CaringBridge site when times are rough. Markus even sometimes posts when things are going well. It is a blessing that others are concerned and care about our son. Readers also have the option to leave comments. Reading through thoughts, well wishes, and expressions of love lifts Markus's spirits.

SWEET PERSONAL NOTES
(TO MARKUS)

Your sitting in silence speaks volumes to a hurting person. Other times, truthful, heartfelt words of encouragement are the best medicine.

Hello Markus!

Remember me??? I want you to know I have been following your CaringBridge entries, and honestly cannot believe what a miracle you are!

Of course, I think you should include something about how awesome it was to have Mrs. Bergh for a teacher for several years but . . .

I have a thousand stories to share about how Markus's smile could light up any room and make my day better. From the days of having a nurse in our classroom to support you, to the *one time* in three years you got in trouble, to realizing you were my parents' neighbor, and then I taught you at home when you could not come to school. However, there is one moment that I remember that has changed the way I work with so many families and students. You do not have to include it, but I thought you (and your parents) might want to hear it.

In your fourth-grade year of school I had a meeting with your mom and dad. They shared with me that it was time for them and for your teachers to *let you be a kid*. We talked about how protective everyone (teachers, custodians, paras) were of our little Markus. I will never forget your dad saying that they and we needed to let you experience life as a kid, without all of us standing around to constantly catch you. We needed to let you fall, to let you make mistakes, to let you simply be a fourth-grade boy.

At first I was terrified. What if something happened to you under my watch? Instead, we observed you learning to navigate so many things independently. Your mom and dad were 100 percent right. *We had to let go so you could get your own wings!* As a teacher I think about that day every single time I have conversations with parents. No matter what labels or obstacles our children have, they are children and we need to let them be just that. Now, as a mom I look at my own child and think of all the things that "could happen." I really do think of you and try to change my thinking to be about what *will* happen when she has the space to just *be*.

Thank you to your whole family for making me a better teacher, and parent.

P.S. I want an autograph once your book is published!

~Mrs. Bergh

▶ ▶ ▶ ▶ ▶

Dear Markus,

Huge congrats and mega best wishes to a young man who has more grit and courage than the old-time Western cowboys.

~D and R

▶ ▶ ▶ ▶ ▶

Way to Go Markus!

I am so proud of you. As I reflect back to your eighth-grade year, I remember all the laughter, effort, and caring you expressed. I knew you would be a super adult—and you are. Way to go, you graduate!

Cheers,

~Mr. G

▸ ▸ ▸ ▸ ▸

Dear Markus,

How exciting to see this big day come! From the time I had you in Sunday school, I saw your inquisitive nature. I cherished the time we spent together.

We are blessed to know you and see you grow into a fine young man. We wish you every blessing as you start college and, as you used to say, "What's next?"!

Love,

~Mr. D and Miss J

▸ ▸ ▸ ▸ ▸

Markus,

It is hard for me to believe you are graduating from high school. I am so proud of everything you have accomplished and the person you have become. I hope you know the powerful impact you have made on our family. My prayer for you is that you continue to grow strong in your faith and seek to serve Him as you pursue the next steps in your life.

Love,

~B, M, A and S

▸ ▸ ▸ ▸ ▸

Dear Markus,

We've been following your progress all your life and are so proud of your accomplishments through trial and test. You have shown such a remarkable spirit and fight, and we are so proud to know you and your example. Blessings in the future.

~The K's

▸ ▸ ▸ ▸ ▸

Markus,

Congratulations on your graduation from high school. I'm certain that not only your parents but also all of your medical caregivers truly appreciate everything you have had to endure to reach this significant milestone in your life. And I'm also certain that as you enter college you will continue striving to reach even greater achievements and successes. Your ongoing strength and courage both are an example to us all, and it strengthens and renews my personal faith in the human spirit.

All the best to you,

~Dr. A

BOOK CLUB DISCUSSION QUESTIONS

1. How do you think God is using Markus in the lives of his family and those around him? Give some examples.

2. Did it surprise you that Markus enjoys hunting and fast cars? Could you sense what joy both brought him? What new thing have you tried lately?

3. How do you feel about Heather and Noah? How are their lives positively and negatively affected by this?

4. In the beginning, Deb is afraid for her marriage, knowing that great stress is about to take place. Mike goes above and beyond to serve his family. Discuss how Mike has influenced Markus's life. How are his actions role models for his other children and for others?

5. Listen to a recording of one of Markus's favorite songs, "Blessings," by Laura Story. What stands out to you?

6. Have you ever had a "Markus" in your life—someone who beat tremendous odds, or have you met someone with an attitude similar to Markus?

7. The Bachman family have received various help from family, neighbors, and friends throughout the years. What are some creative ways you could help others in need? Is there anyone in your life that you could serve right now?

8. What kinds of trials have you had in your life, and how did you work through them?

CPSIA information can be obtained
at www.ICGtesting.com
Printed in the USA
LVHW040604161120
671798LV00002B/212

9 781946 195654